Friend to Mankind

Marsilio Ficino (1433–1499)

Happy Christmas Sweetheart,
and a happy New Year.
with love,
Jonathan.

Friend to Mankind

Marsilio Ficino (1433–1499)

Michael Shepherd
EDITOR

SHEPHEARD-WALWYN

First published 1999 by
Shepheard-Walwyn (Publishers) Ltd
26 Charing Cross Road (Suite 34)
London WC2H 0DH

British Library Cataloguing in Publication Data

A catalogue record of this book
is available from the British Library

ISBN 0 85683 184 0

Typeset by R E Clayton
Printed in Great Britain by St Edmundsbury Press,
Bury St Edmunds, Suffolk

Contents

Foreword

SINCE fluency in Latin and Greek has decreased during the 20th century, particularly in the English-speaking world, the very existence of this volume owes a great debt to those who have translated and written about Marsilio Ficino in English: first and foremost, to Paul Oskar Kristeller, who died aged 94 in 1999, and who was the leading authority in bringing Ficino back to the attention of philosophers. Then to Sears Jayne, whose 1944 translation of *De Amore* revealed the profound influence of Ficino's doctrine of universal love on the arts and literature; to Carol Kaske and John Clarke for their translation of *De Vita*, Ficino's most intriguing work for contemporary therapeutics; to Michael Allen, for his ongoing translations and researches into every aspect of Ficino's thought, particularly the commentaries on Plato's dialogues; and to the team working through Ficino's twelve books of letters, which reveal the inspirational aspect of Ficino's activities.

Gratitude, too, to the memory of Norah Fillingham, whose Christian devotion and inspired elegance of phrase gave wings to the English translation of the letters from the beginning.

Introduction

*It is not for small things but for great that God created men,
who, knowing the great, are not satisfied with small things.
Indeed, it is for the limitless alone that He created men, who
are the only beings on earth to have re-discovered their
infinite nature and who are not fully satisfied by anything
limited however great that thing may be.* *

THIS passage, tucked away in a letter to one of his friends, offers the
perfect introduction to Marsilio Ficino for those unfamiliar with his
writings. It indicates why the 500th anniversary of his lifetime should
be cause for celebration; and reason for his rediscovery as one of the
great and timeless 'friends of mankind'.

For he is one of those rare beings who seem to be born with the
welfare of the whole human race as their prime concern; and he
expresses this with love, authority, scholarship, poetic imagination
and sublime eloquence.

Re-reading that quotation, we can perhaps begin to imagine –
difficult historical exercise though this is – what it was like for men
and women of his own time to hear such inspiring, expansive words
for the first time. Their tone is not obviously Judaic, Greek, Roman,
Christian or Islamic; yet it harmonises the transcendent teachings of
all these traditions, and restates their universal message in a fresh and
invigorating way; and with all the authority of personal experience.

It was writings such as this, from his villa at Careggi overlooking
Florence – and personal contact too, for Ficino delivered sermons as a
priest, gave lectures, supervised an academy, wrote letters and is said
to have been loved by young and old in his day for his conversation –

*Ficino, *Letters*, Vol 4, letter 6

which helped to awaken those surging energies, in many fields of human interest and discovery, which we so marvel at and call the Renaissance.

The last half-century has yielded a considerable scholarly literature concerning Ficino (a guide to further reading will be found at the back of this volume), which has established his historical significance: first as translator of Plato and other philosophers from Greek; as highly influential commentator on these; as harmoniser of classical 'paganism' and Christianity; and whose writings led to the adoption of the belief in the immortality of the soul as Christian dogma; but beyond that, as a voice in his own right, a teacher of mankind, no less.

His influence can be traced – in England and in the idealistic New World as much as anywhere – through the succeeding centuries, as theologian and philosopher (though himself believing these two terms ultimately to be one), and poetic voice of transcendent love, human and divine; inspiring poets and artists with a new, many-layered language of imagination; and providing the new sciences with psychology – literally, the knowledge of the soul.

For those who wish to discover the golden thread of our Western tradition – which ultimately must be the tradition of truth itself – Ficino is an excellent point of entry. The image which fits him well is that of the hourglass: in the upper cup, the whole of the cultural inheritance of the Mediterranean from Egypt, Israel, Persia and beyond, Greece, Rome, Byzantium and Islam; and from medieval Europe itself. Then at the narrow neck of the hourglass, Ficino himself, filtering and discriminating grain by grain all this – word and truth, wisdom and speculation. And in the cup below, the fine tilth of culture which his work provided, a seed-bed for the work of others to come. Following up the authors cited and references in his letters, for instance (the easiest starting point, as he himself intended), can take one deep into this Western tradition and the unimaginable riches of the finest thought and the greatest minds.

This invitation to live a greater life was received with eager enthusiasm throughout Europe even during his lifetime, by kings, prelates, scholars and artists. But what of the present day? Has Marsilio Ficino anything to say to us today worth listening to? Can he still inspire us to believe ourselves greater than our thoughts?

It may come as a surprise to some readers that for a quarter of a century now, in the New World, Ficino has provided an inspiration and method for practising psychotherapists, and a spiritual guide in everyday living; notably in the books of Dr Thomas Moore. It is a merry thought that in America – named after the nephew of one of Ficino's friends and correspondents – Ficino's name is more widely known than in Europe at this time.

To return to this question of Ficino for today: the answer lies with the reader. Here is a test: on reading that quotation which heads this introduction, is there a warm response – whether 'That's true' or 'That's what I'd like to believe'? If there is that warmth, it suggests two things in particular: that it was written from personal experience, not just from convenient idealist theory; and more, that our response proves that we ourselves already know this greatness, this unbounded nature, within ourselves. It is reminding us of what we are. As Ficino says elsewhere, we are essentially that which is greatest within us – which he calls the soul. All his writings are an invitation to all mankind, to live as that greater self; to think and act and love universally, as heirs of the whole Creation; and to find joy in this. His essential message is both profound and practical: the joy, the freedom, of seeking answers to all questions from the viewpoint of the unity of all things. As Ficino himself says, only the unlimited truly satisfies us.

This book of celebratory essays is written by some of those who have rediscovered Marsilio Ficino and have come to love him as a teacher and a friend; so its structure is relaxed and personal. But it aims to celebrate three aspects of Ficino's value over five hundred years, as suggested above: his inspiration in his own times; his extending influence in subsequent centuries and in many directions; and most of all, his continuing practical relevance today. The essays follow this order.

Two mental images of the one Ficino may emerge from these essays; and they affect the mind in different ways. One is of Ficino the embodiment: the person, the actuality. As with his patron Cosimo de' Medici, he appears on the scene at a crucial time; realises what needs to be done; does it; and then leaves the stage of history, his role fulfilled. The other image – almost an imageless image – is of Ficino the shared mind: the writings, the conversations we will never hear, the Ficino who lives on, to be rediscovered and to influence new generations in new ways. Adrian Bertoluzzi, who is currently working on a biography of Marsilio Ficino, provides here an account of Ficino the embodiment: the main events of his life, and the role he played in those vibrant and turbulent times. From the sober details of a quiet life emerges the quintessence of the Renaissance and of Ficino's significance: one man in his microcosm studying the macrocosm, the whole Creation; the individual seeking the universal.

One virtue which the younger generation seems to be carrying into the new millennium is that of compassion – both for the planet and for its inhabitants. Compassion cannot be manufactured; it arises naturally out of observation and heartfelt understanding, and may then move toward contemplation, action or creative work. Clement Salaman in the second essay focusses on Ficino's compassion, and shows how this compassion spread into all these areas so effectively.

One, Two, Three: Plato's and Plotinus' search for the One unity; the Eastern principle of non-dualism or *advaita* (or in Western theology, non-contradiction); and the Christian mystery of the Trinity: each of these presents a method and a challenge to the thinking of theologians, philosophers, mystics and anyone who takes up this adventure in thought. Arthur Farndell, a student of Ficino's philosophy and of *advaita*, assembles Ficino's most inspiring statements on unity, setting them out by theme and context, and translating some passages into English for the first time.

The names of Pico della Mirandola and Poliziano (Politian as he was often known in Britain) have both been celebrated over subsequent centuries as stars, young lions of the Renaissance – more so than Ficino; yet there is no modern biography of either at the moment of writing, and their letters – including those to Ficino himself, with all their inherent fascination – mostly await translation. Linda Proud brings these two young men out of the wings to share the spotlight along with Ficino as they did in their own times, giving a sense of the ferment of discussion and new ideas which must have gone on in Florence and beyond; played out against the turbulent backdrop of the times and the personal risks of murderous politics and the bonfires of heresy which attended new thinking. Indeed, both men died young, and some suspected poisoning. What emerges from this account is that ardent love of enquiry and truth which was their bond of friendship, and which must have been that much more intense at the time of the 'new learning'.

With men of stature such as Marsilio Ficino it is easy, in the half-light of hindsight, to underestimate or overestimate them; to adulate them or to cut them down to our size. This is understandable. An effective philosopher will inspire equally in society, action, devotion and knowledge; and speak truth in different 'voices' according to his audience. This is so with Ficino; indeed, it was familiar practice in his day. In his writing we can hear sometimes a respectful regard for tradition, discriminating but uncritical; or close informative paraphrasing of the words of Augustine, Aquinas or – from his own translating – Plato, Plotinus, Hermes Trismegistus, pseudo-Dionysius, Proclus and others. In some treatises a closely argued 'Aristotelian' tone may be set against a transcendental 'Platonic' tone, which can be as much from his own experience and intuition as direct from Plato or the neo-Platonists. In the letters it is the voice of eternal unity, friendship and love, most often, with inspirational intent; which can rise to an exalted voice of ecstatic 'divine frenzy', where the poet and the seer meet. There is humour, levity, word-play and teasing too. To his superiors in the priesthood Ficino adopts the traditional tone of fulsome respect which we might term unctuous flattery (though with more than a touch of irony when his 'superior' is a 16-year old bishop or cardinal, or a scheming, warlike Pope); and to rulers and princes, an equally fulsome tone of unstinted praise. But this should not be misunderstood as 'crawly': Marsilio is speaking to the office itself in its power and duty, and to the man as he should be, whether priest or ruler. Beyond this he is speaking to the divine in all men, as his 'friends in unity'. This is the most elevating aspect of Ficino's letters.

Alas, we seldom have the written response to the letters – though research may yet find some. However, Valery Rees presents the evidence, beginning with a detailed account of the scene in Hungary, of the way in which Ficino's correspondents and followers spread his ideas, thought and teaching through Europe. It is a fascinating story, even instructive, and which the subsequent essays follow up. Behind it all lies the abiding mystery: the power that launches and transmits such a renaissance.

For Ficino, philosophy, the love of wisdom, is essentially a practical matter, through the pursuit of which we can come to know our real selves, and rest the mind at last in that knowledge. In his *Theologia Platonica* he explains this process in terms of contemplation, by which the mind withdraws itself from the body, and from ' all obstacles of the senses and fantasy', and finds all the treasures of knowledge already there within itself. In his *De Amore*, his commentary on Plato's *Symposium* which became greatly influential in its own right, Ficino expounds the role of love and beauty in this return of the soul to its divine self. Joseph Milne's lucid and penetrating study presents Ficino's views in both their Platonic and Christian context, and takes us to the very heart of Ficino's teaching.

When Ficino embarked on his great harmonisation of Plato and Christianity, reason and revelation, he could have chosen to disregard as irrelevant those two extraordinary areas of thought: mythology and astrology. And he would have had Church authority for thus dismissing them from consideration. But in his unifying cosmic view, he chose to investigate both, to see what they would yield in observable or intuitive truth about the 'heavens within'; with results which laid the ground for the development of psychology, the knowledge of the soul, as the later essays in this volume reveal. Geoffrey Pearce sets out Ficino's views and pronouncements on astrology, in the context of his times. In this, Ficino's letters are as valuable as his better-known treatises in providing clues as to his theory and practice. His guiding principle, as it was for Origen and others, was the correspondence, in a unified Creation, between the outer and the inner.

The first authorities in recent times to bring Ficino's name back to general attention were art historians who were also philosophers:

Professors Cassirer, Panofsky, Kristeller, Garin, Chastel, Wind, Saxl, Wittkower and Gombrich have all made distinguished contributions in this field. The many-layered language of the imagination which Ficino was to bequeath to artistic imagery can be seen prefigured in the most 'playful' of his letters: for instance, that short note to Phoebus (Febo) Capella of Venice in Volume 6 of the English translation, where Ficino brings together five levels of reference – physical or astronomical, astrological, mythological, celestial or psychological and personal – through his light-hearted word-play (as with Shakespeare later) and loving allusion. The possibilities that this opened up for visual artists are revealed by the great art galleries and private collections of the world in all their glory; from the most spiritually serious in intent to the most decoratively light-hearted. Pamela Tudor-Craig, whose study of Botticelli's relationship to Ficino in her book *The Secret Life of Paintings* is deeply stimulating, focusses here on one aspect of Renaissance art less often discussed in philosophic context: the painted portrait in its most profound application, as the meeting of the specifically personal and the eternal in the living soul. (Were it not so hackneyed, a reproduction of Leonardo's 'Mona Lisa' would be entirely appropriate here.)

1999 marks another 500th anniversary, curiously interlinked, even to the month, with Ficino's death. In that month, October 1499, three great men, all just beginning their public careers, met in Oxford. John Colet was embarking on a series of public lectures on St Paul's *Epistles*; he had written two letters to Marsilio Ficino, one of admiration for his writings, particularly *The Letters*, which had been published in Venice as recently as 1495; the second letter probably (he did not keep a copy) asking about the respective powers of intellect and will in the journey of the soul to God. Later, as Dean of St Paul's Cathedral, Colet was to preach mighty sermons in front of Henry VIII, Wolsey and the convocation of England's priests. Desiderius Erasmus, the second of this trio, was to become the great Bible scholar of Europe; the third was Thomas More, destined to become Henry VIII's adviser, friend, enemy and victim. In 1499 Colet and Erasmus were in their early thirties and More in his early twenties; they delighted in each other's company, the more so as they all shared a sense of humour. In this we might see that unique quality of the English Renaissance, its blend of humour, humanism and humanity which reached its height in Shakespeare. These three men have become known as the 'Oxford Reformers'. Bearing in mind the corruption of the Church and Papacy at the time, and Erasmus' comment that Rome behaved 'as if Christ were dead', it would not be too far-fetched or fanciful to claim in that same spirit that Jesus Christ was resurrected in Oxford in 1499. Jenifer Capper sets Colet and Ficino and their relationship (Colet the only English correspondent of Ficino, though one or two others such as Grocyn and Linacre might have met him during their studies in Florence) in the context of their times and aims.

As the Renaissance spread by word of mouth and pen, and the oxygen of expanding awareness, through Europe from South to North, each nation, as international Latin declined, brought forth a national genius in its new native language – Luther, Rabelais, Cervantes, Hooft, Camoens, Shakespeare. Shakespeare's debt to Ficino has been obscured for us by his sheer genius – transmuting philosophic gold into poetic gold with a lightning-swift intuitive understanding of the most profound thought which makes the term 'influence' almost irrelevant: the origin, the aim, the effect is one. Jill Line points to the direct parallels between Shakespeare's philosophic poetry and Ficino's poetic philosophy in an essay which illumines and deepens the study of both writers.

Ficino's most expansive influence is to be seen in the arts, particularly the visual and literary arts. Less identifiable, but perhaps greater than has been realised, is his influence on music. He himself set great value on the use of music in healing - as did Pythagoras. He was a practising musician and extemporiser in song and on the lyre as well as confident theorist, as in his letter to Domenico Benivieni expounding the mathematical and philosophical basis of the modern octave. Alas, we know nothing of the practice; except that it was said to be effective. The authority of that letter, and the similar section on music in his *Timaeus* commentary, may have had a wide and immediate response, or a gradual one – we cannot be sure. Both treatises bear considerable contemplation, even today. Certainly the principle that musical harmony, like the soul, is the connection between the human and the divine, and therefore of universal and vital influence, must have struck home. Ficino's rich language of imagination on several levels, combined with his emphasis on the cosmic harmony reflected in music, gives him a claim to be a significant figure in the birth of opera which followed the elaborate cosmic masques of Italian courts and, later, those of Inigo Jones and Ben Jonson for the English court. John Allitt pays tribute to the considerable influence which he believes Ficino to have had on music.

There is so much to learn – to rediscover, recognise, acknowledge, remember – in Ficino's writings. It is thus a particular delight and encouragement to the translators of his letters and other works, when specialists of our own day find what he says to be relevant and inspiring. L.L.Blake highlights, from the point of view of a barrister and writer on law, Ficino's personal pronouncements on the levels and aspects of law, and the relationship to justice. He links this to the contribution which the principles underpinning the Common Law of England can make in the current debate on Europe and sovereignty.

Few gain a more intimate acquaintance with the very thought of great writers and thinkers than those who are called upon to translate their words: a spiritual bond which takes the mind beyond language in order to find language. Ficino's deep understanding of the thought of Plato and Plotinus and other Greek minds arose through his being the first translator of most of their works into Latin. The same spiritual bond has arisen between Ficino and his translators into English – not surprisingly, since his themes are above all friendship, love and unity. Patricia Gillies writes about the developing experience of translating Ficino's letters, its subtleties and its spiritual rewards.

As mentioned earlier, Ficino's name is more widely known in the United States than in Europe thanks to a quarter-century of practical application of his thought and vision to psychotherapy and daily life. This has gained a wide audience through the books of Dr Thomas Moore, such as *Care of the Soul* and *The Planets Within*, which have brought Ficino's insights into the life and context of today. Dr Moore contributes from his experience an essay on Ficino as magus and cultural visionary; a splendid justification of this celebration of 'Ficino 500'.

Ficino, the son of a doctor, also trained as a doctor and inherited the medieval tradition of linking astrology, music and medicine in the holistic pursuit of health. To this he brought his own cosmic view, and his *Three Books on Life* together with his other writings on these subjects deserve contemporary expert and open-minded study. Dr Charlotte Mendes da Costa contributes a fascinating survey of Ficino's views and advice: as a practising doctor she finds much contemporary relevance which could stimulate further professional discussion. It is interesting that, all of five centuries on, we can begin once again to consider the links between the spiritual, the emotional, the mental and the physical in terms of professional practice. It is also tantalising that Ficino's own practice of using music with medicine remains un-documented – a whole field of research awaits.

One authority on Ficino, Michael Allen, has pointed out that the 20th century has an affinity with the 15th in its open-mindedness. This has encouraged investigation of the practical relevance of Ficino's insights in today's world of the soul. Noel Cobb is one of the distinguished few in Britain who have paralleled the work of James Hillman and Thomas Moore in America over the last quarter-century in applying these insights to psychotherapy – or, to use Ficino's more direct word, life, in particular the life of the soul. Noel Cobb contributes a richly imaginative dialogue between Ficino and a present-day practitioner of this soul-healing, which illuminates this fruitful collaboration over the centuries, bringing the past into the present in a way which would surely make Ficino himself rejoice.

Ficino travelled no further from Florence for most of his life than the hills around it; yet through his conversations, letters and books, he was in touch with kings and powerful rulers, popes and prelates, statesmen and politicians, lawyers, scholars, poets, musicians, writers and artists – decision-makers and creators, all leaders in their field. David Boddy, who meets many such leaders, and young potential leaders, in the course of his work, takes up the theme of leadership –

on which Ficino offers such penetrating and uncompromising advice – and applies it to the world as it is today.

During the preparation of this volume, a major event occurred in the Western Church: Pope John Paul II issued his Encyclical Letter *Fides et Ratio* on faith and reason. How this would have rejoiced Ficino – on behalf of the whole of mankind! He lived in a time of extreme corruption in the Papacy and in the Church in general, as well as knowing the perils of the Inquisition and the burning of alleged heretics; but here is a Pope affirming that there is one absolute truth which philosophy and religion must meet together to seek; that every human being has an 'implicit philosophy', a desire placed in the human heart to know the truth; that this is the path by which we may come to know ourselves; and that we can come to that understanding through the things we know best, the things of everyday life. His Holiness calls philosophy 'an indispensible help for the deeper understanding of faith' and he frees our minds of any limiting ideas about signing up to some defined faith and dogma by indicating that real faith is a total surrender to the infinite and the absolute. His Holiness has a special word for Indian thought, in liberating the spirit from the 'shackles of time and space'; and when he affirms that 'The desire for knowledge is so great and it works in such a way that the human heart, despite its experience of insurmountable limitation, yearns for the infinite riches which lie beyond, knowing that there is to be found the satisfying answer to every question as yet unanswered' – this evokes the same sound as that of Ficino's statement which heads this introduction. The Reverend Professor Serracino-Inglott, who, like St Augustine, Marsilio Ficino and Pope John Paul, is both priest and philosopher, considers Ficino to be 'an unacknowledged precursor in the formulation of much needed Christian concepts and attitudes in the world of today'; his resonant essay on Ficino's message to the Church today establishes in the widest and most profound terms why we should be celebrating Marsilio Ficino as a man of this and the next millennium. It brings this volume to a fitting conclusion.

These essays reveal the vast scope of human – and divine – concerns which can arise from an acquaintance with Marsilio Ficino. Were the volume a full view of his significance, it would happily include longer essays from all its contributors; also ideally, at least three other areas of investigation. One, rather more historical but full of interest, is the way in which the vision of the loving unity of Creation held by Ficino and others who shared his vision, contributed to the development of modern science: how insight, speculation, even astrology and mythology, prepared the way for observation, hypothesis, experiment and discovery of physical and chemical laws. Copernicus, Brahe, Galileo, Kepler and Newton all figure in this story.

A second area, already touched on in these essays, is nearer home: the considerable influence of Ficino's thought through centuries of English – and American – literature and theatre (to mention only one language and two nations among several). Most apparent is its transmutation by genius in Shakespeare, yet most difficult to pin down. The very profundity of Ficino's vision makes it all the more elusive to us, its heirs. But it is worth investigation since, like all true study, it is ultimately a study of oneself. Thomas Traherne's response, in his *Centuries of Meditations*, to this call to a universal view, with the need to pass on the recognition of this cosmic inheritance to children at an early age, is just one shining glory in our literature in which Ficino played a part.

The third area of interest would require a whole volume of itself. Fortunately, it has been very deeply researched in Professor Kristeller's *The Philosophy of Marsilio Ficino*: to wit, the very core of Ficino's thought and exposition, especially that most practical aspect which Kris-teller calls 'internal experience' or consciousness. Ficino's *Theologia Platonica* represents his most fully developed teaching. Its theoretical and practical importance is shown by the fact that most of the ample quotations in Kristeller's book are from the *Theologia*. So, for a sustained presentation of Ficino's full view of Creation and the role of mankind in it – set down in eighteen 'books' at the age of 36-41 – readers are commended, until the *Theologia* is translated, to Kristeller's volume. Michael Allen in his books and essays investigates the development of Ficino's thought in his life subsequent to the *Theologia* – twenty-five years which saw Ficino's translations of and commentaries on Synesius, Iamblicus, Psellus, Priscian, Porphyry, Proclus, Plotinus, Dionysius, Athenagoras and St Paul's *Epistles*, among others; and his revised commentaries to Plato's dialogues such as *Philebus*, *Phaedrus* and *Sophist* intended for his second edition of Plato in 1496.

A fourth area of interest could launch another renaissance in itself, matching that flowing from the work of Ficino, Pico and others, and continuing this: to harmonise the vast treasures of Vedic wisdom and the Sanskrit language with our Western tradition. The essays by Arthur Farndell and Joseph Milne hint at this; the translators of Ficino's letters have frequently found that recourse to a Sanskrit dictionary and *Dhatupatha* have aided the penetration of Ficino's etymologies and thought through language. It is not only the holy grail of *prisca theologia* which shines beyond this search: such study throws light on both Eastern and Western traditions. Experts have pointed out that Eastern languages are generally richer in their vocabulary for the mental and spiritual worlds than are Western; if this be so, an exciting field of research beckons.

Marsilio Ficino's intellectual contribution to Western culture is vast, clearing blockages and opening up the mind. Spiritually, he revealed the path of personal development which, though inherent in all teachings, may for many have appeared closed. Indeed, it could be claimed that the 20th century could not have thought to discuss 'self-realisation' without the encouragement of Ficino to find the universal within the individual, and unity in diversity, in the 15th century. The 500th anniversary of Ficino's lifetime – and also of his impact on the 'Oxford Reformers' – falls on the eve of the new millennium for Western mankind – arithmetically, at least. But *if* mankind is evolutionary, then, two thousand years after the birth of Christ and two-and-a-half thousand years after the glory that was Greece, ought we not to be surrounded by a mighty chorus of priests, philosophers, politicians, economists, lawyers, artists, scientists, psychologists, story-tellers and all the media, reminding us of the greatness of the human race, and demanding of us that we confront this individual greatness within ourselves; in that hunger for the unlimited, that desire and pursuit of the whole of which Marsilio Ficino speaks so ardently?

This volume is a celebration of just one such voice: a voice of love, wisdom, authority, scholarship, poetic imagination and sublime eloquence, which still calls us to seek that greater life and know ourselves.

Finally, a brief personal testimony. The writer was studying one of Ficino's letters – in a London Underground train, of all places – when he was suddenly overcome by the most profound spiritual illumination that he had yet experienced, full of detail and meaning, personal and universal; a view of the world from the eternal perfection of the soul itself. It left him in no doubt that Ficino's voice holds the same power today as it did five hundred years ago; yet the interpretation was fresh and new. Such a spiritual illumination is surely one of the greatest gifts that any human being can ever pass on to another human being? As Ficino himself might put it, it is giving oneself back to oneself.

It is in this spirit that this volume of celebration is offered: to beloved Marsilio Ficino in his immortal self; to those many other established 'friends of Marsilio' old and new; and to generations of future friends yet to meet him. *Vale atque Ave.*

Michael Shepherd
Editor

Marsilio Ficino - A Man for All Seasons

ADRIAN BERTOLUZZI

Sow...this arid field of humankind with good will,
and it will at length not only abound with fruit and vines,
but also flow with milk and honey. *

IN THE bright firmament of the Italian Renaissance no luminary has suffered in recent times a more unmerited eclipse than Marsilio Ficino. Today in Florence anyone can freely admire the majestic grace of Brunelleschi's cupola. Ficino left no such tangible testimony of his life's work. The influence he bequeathed to posterity was celebrated under the sacrosanct names of Plato, Plotinus, Hermes Trismegistus and Dionysius the Areopagite. But during his lifetime which spanned sixty-six years Ficino was hailed as something of a legend in his own right; recognised as a philosopher, musician and doctor, a healer of souls; celebrated in poetry as a new Orpheus, who once wrote 'May the well tempered lyre always be our salvation when we apply ourselves to it rightly'.[1]

Virtually all his writings were published in his lifetime including his correspondence in twelve books which is an impressive testimony to the wide circle of friends drawn to this 'Marsyas' of the Renaissance.[2]

Ficino clearly had all the makings of a master teacher: one word, one smile would suffice to soften the heart of even the most hardened sceptic. A magnetic personality; disarming in his forthrightness and simplicity of manners, vast in the breadth and scope of his learning; a prodigiously retentive memory. His charming innocence, universal compassion and thirst for true knowledge mark him out as a teacher in

* Ficino, *Letters*, Vol 1, p.117, to Lorenzo de Medici.

the great traditions of religious and philosophical sages who embrace the one universal truth.

At this time there was a concerted impulse to heal the divisions within society which had festered for so long. Ficino was indeed aware of two forces at work in society, the material and the spiritual; these spring from the nature of the soul which has a dual aspect. As he says in one letter, the soul is set on a horizon midway between the eternal and the temporal: 'it is capable of rational power and action which lead up to the eternal but also of energies and activities which descend to the temporal'.[3] When either of these two halves are ignored or neglected so that they appear to be at odds with one another, society tends inevitably to run down and become fragmented; divisions and rifts manifest with greater force and frequency. According to Ficino the remedy for this malaise is self knowledge which brings these two aspects once more into clear focus and into accord: 'thus the Delphic injunction "know thyself" is fulfilled and we examine everything else, whether above or beneath the soul, with deeper insight'. Ficino's or rather Plato's teachings provided this very insight; and with these two sides of man's nature fully acknowledged again, a healing process was set in motion; equilibrium was being restored to society, and the very same century that had witnessed such acts of intolerance as the persecution of the Hussites and the burning at the stake of John Huss and Jerome of Prague, also saw the ending of the long schism which had divided the church between Avignon and Rome, and experienced a great outpouring of creativity in all the arts, that miraculous reawakening of the human spirit vividly described in Ficino's own words as a golden age, one that brings forth golden minds in abundance, a spirit which is still present to us five hundred years on.

Marsilio Ficino was the second son of Diotifeci Ficino, who became a personal physician to Cosimo de Medici, head of the richest and most powerful family in Florence, bankers to a succession of Popes.

Cosimo was to play a crucial role in Ficino's resolve to devote his life to philosophy. Himself a man of heroic resolve: as witnessed in his confrontation with the powerful Albizzi faction, his imprisonment, exile and triumphant return to Florence one year later (1434) as undisputed ruler. Adversity had made him single-minded and resolute: as Ficino would say, the spirit is tried and made strong in adversity as gold is purified in fire.[4] Cosimo's extraordinary love of the classical world, its art and literature, showed itself early in his life when he tried to visit the Holy Land in search of manuscripts. Later he would become one of the most discerning and generous patrons in history. But he was also drawn to philosophy. Ever since a providential meeting with the Byzantine philosopher Gemistos Plethon, regarded as the living embodiment of Plato himself, which took place at the Council of Florence in 1439, Cosimo was so fired by this philosopher's account of Plato's Academy and teachings, that it became his one overriding wish to restore Plato's philosophy to Italy. An early meeting with Ficino when he was still a young boy had raised his expectations that here was someone who might have the potential to accomplish this task. It was his second and decisive meeting with Ficino, now a university student, that finally convinced Cosimo he had made the right judgment. Ficino had just embarked on a course in medicine, intending to make it his life's career in deference to the wishes of his father, but in a dramatic intervention Cosimo recalled Ficino to the study of philosophy and the healing of souls. Ficino's conversations with Cosimo on philosophy began from this time forward, and a deep bond of friendship based on mutual trust was forged between the two men. Cosimo was now taking a close interest in Ficino's studies and even encouraged some of his early writings, including an introduction to Plato and his philosophy based mainly on Latin authors, but Cosimo advised Ficino to master the Greek language and 'drink from the source' before proceeding further with his study of Plato.

When Ficino had mastered Greek and had translated some key texts including the oracles of Zoroaster and the hymns of Orpheus, Cosimo commissioned Ficino to translate the whole of Plato (1462), giving him a volume containing Plato's *Dialogues* in Greek; the Platonic Academy of Florence was set up at this time, probably to coincide with this commission. The real purpose of this so called Academy was to teach Plato's philosophy as a way of life; gatherings of like-minded friends met within its walls, with Ficino defining true friendships as a fellowship between those men pursuing the same goal - the virtue of wisdom.

At about the same time a school modelled on the Athenian Lyceum where Aristotle taught was established under John Argyropoulos a disciple of Plethon's. Its purpose seems to have been to study the writings of Aristotle as a preparation for the Platonic teachings. This venture also had Cosimo's support.

Around 1463 Cosimo suddenly interrupted Ficino's work on Plato, giving him a new commission, to translate a manuscript which had just come to light containing writings of Hermes Trismegistus, an Egyptian priest and sage, believed by ancient authors to have lived at the time of Moses, and to have imparted his secret teachings to Moses. Later these teachings had passed to the Greek Orpheus, whence they had also been handed on to Pythagoras and Plato. Ficino was convinced that the Hebrew and Greek wisdom sprang from a common ancestry.

Just before Cosimo's death in 1464, Ficino presented him with his translation of ten of the shorter dialogues of Plato; and as if to mark this happy event, in a letter to Cosimo Ficino declared that the spirit of Plato, alive in his writings, had flown from Athens to Florence to be with Cosimo.[5] On hearing these dialogues read to him for the first time Cosimo was overjoyed, realising that Plato's philosophy had finally reached Italy.[6]

Cosimo's son Piero, the 'Gouty' who succeeded him, was weak and ineffectual due to ill-health. The period he was in power was overshadowed by plots and instability, but Piero supported Ficino and remained loyal to the spirit of Cosimo. He encouraged Ficino to continue his work on Plato and to give public lectures on Plato's philosophy which were held in the University. These lectures were important because they opened out the teachings for the first time to a wider audience. Ficino had almost completed a first draft of his translations of Plato on Piero's death in 1469. But a further period of uncertainty followed whilst power was being transferred to his son Lorenzo de' Medici. Ficino describes this time as one when 'envious fortune' interrupted his work on Plato.[7] Uncertain whether the young Lorenzo would be capable of establishing his political authority and giving his full backing to the Academy, it seems Ficino visited Rome in search of potential new patrons. This coincided with a hotly debated controversy over the respective merits of Plato and Aristotle between Cardinal Bessarion and George of Trebizond. But Bessarion, a former pupil of Plethon's and a staunch ally of Ficino's, saved the day in his exemplary defence of Plato published in 1469. This work marked an important milestone in getting Plato's moral teachings accepted as being in harmony with Christian values and as a powerful medium to educate society. Bessarion was a leading authority on Plato, being one of the few men in Italy to possess a volume of all his *Dialogues* in Greek, and he made full use of the new invention of printing recently introduced into Italy.

This prepared the stage for the next phase, expounding the spiritual heart of Plato's philosophy within the Academy, which took place in Florence under the protection of Lorenzo de' Medici. Lorenzo became a pillar of the Academy both in the financial support he gave and in his own active participation. This work of the Academy was to continue for the next twenty years under Ficino's direction. Members included some of the closest friends and supporters of the Medici who were actively involved in government and this gave the Academy more authority and influence. In these early years of Lorenzo's rule, activities of the Academy were conducted quite openly and meetings were held in the Medici villas; also under the auspices of a lay confraternity patronised by the Medici, the Confraternity of the Magi.

In his letters Ficino appears to endow Lorenzo with heroic qualities which acted as a reminder of those qualities he really possessed and which should be made manifest.[8] At his best, according to Ficino, Lorenzo gave each of the three Graces their due: Venus – poetry and the arts; Juno – power and government; and Minerva – wisdom.[9] But there were two sides to Lorenzo's personality; on the one hand he was a gifted poet, diplomat and statesman, a promoter of fine causes; on the other he could be proud, ambitious and impulsive; negative qualities reflected in his choice of friends. Whereas in the early years of his rule Lorenzo devoted much time to the Academy and Ficino, as the business of government grew more demanding, and claimed more of his attention, this diminished and a rift of sorts developed between the two men. Lorenzo became estranged from Ficino especially in the period leading up to the Pazzi Conspiracy. Ficino's close association with Lorenzo became the butt of slanderous jibes and insinuations from the pen of certain members of Lorenzo's own court circle; the Academy was also under attack. Foremost among these was the satirical poet Luigi Pulci – the 'flea' a favourite with the Medici for the comic relief he provided at table. Pulci was a buffoon who liked pranks and stirring up trouble of all sorts. To him the serious study of philosophy was incomprehensible. Pulci wrote a gargantuan poem *Morgante*, based on a Carolingian epic about Charlemagne's court and his knights, full of absurd situations and bizarre characters one of whom is called 'Marsilius', a treacherous infidel King of Spain who comes to a sticky end in the final canto. Later Pulci's poem, which also satirises religious belief, had the dubious distinction of being burnt on one of Savonarola's bonfires of vanities.

Ficino was not one to be troubled by a flea like Pulci. He had a remarkable sense of humour of his own and he could turn adverse situations like this one to advantage. His witty sayings in Tuscan were proverbial and were remembered long after his time. All that really concerned Ficino was the influence that the likes of Pulci could have on Lorenzo. Whilst Pulci's sonnets caricatured Ficino and the Academy, the Academy parried with sonnets of its own; but as this episode occurred at a difficult time for Ficino, some of Pulci's sonnets must have seemed like the last straw:

Marsilio this philosophy of yours n'er heard
from the lips of any mortal.
You put it to rest at nones
only to spout it forth again in babble and lunacy.
Thus the prophecy comes true
your lyre to utter : play me, play me!
Sonnets to me? Sonnets to you I say.
You poke a fire! let it scorch you,
you'll have it up your backside ere long.

Horrid pipsqueak!
lop off the blockhead, dock his tail!
What sayest thou? What translatest?
Plato! a plague on him and you as well.
Swearest an oath upon philosophy!
Nani, Nani! (dwarf)
one day at Careggi you spouted forth so much
that wilt have no more to say unless thou mug'st up more.[10]

Ficino was able to brush off the slanderous jibes of the 'flea' Pulci; but the Pazzi Conspiracy to oust the Medici from Florence which had the Pope's backing, represented a very serious challenge not only to Lorenzo and the Republic but also to the Academy itself, probably the greatest threat faced by the Academy at any time during its existence. If the plot had succeeded it is hard to see how the work of the Academy could have continued. Following the failure of the coup, Lorenzo was excommunicated by the Pope, and the Florentine Republic was surrounded by a hostile alliance of states. Yet, according to the French envoy, Lorenzo's sole crime in the eyes of his enemies had been his failure to get himself assassinated.[11]

Ficino remained in the background during this critical period, although his passivity was questioned by at least one of his friends, the Venetian Ambassador Bernardo Bembo. But he did play a key role behind the scenes: two magnificent orations were addressed to Pope Sixtus IV, the main adversary of Florence, as well as an oracle to King Ferdinand of Naples in the cause of peace;[12] and Ficino almost certainly gave advice to Lorenzo who faced further conspiracies against his life and who found himself universally blamed by friends and family alike for attracting so much hostility against the Republic, with the Medici Bank on the verge of collapse and the City of Florence on the verge of starvation. But Lorenzo's courageous and impromptu mission to Naples to detach Ferdinand from the hostile alliance saved the day. Because Ficino had corresponded with two of the main conspirators and had most probably received financial support from them, and the fact that a third conspirator had been a long standing member of the

Academy, Ficino was himself suspected of complicity in the plot and was under investigation. Indeed it is thought Ficino even briefly considered leaving Florence to join one of his Roman patrons. But the whole crisis, far from alienating Lorenzo still further from Ficino, actually brought the two men closer together. During this period Ficino wrote some of his most inspired and moving letters to Lorenzo, one on the unity of their guardian spirit, and another on the harmony between country life and city life represented by Saturn and Apollo, the two aspects of daily life that Lorenzo found so difficult to bring together.

In the late 1480s Lorenzo was completely reconciled with the Academy and during the last part of his life he seemed to reach a new level of understanding and humanity, fully justifying the heroic praises lavished on him in the beginning by Ficino. One letter of Ficino's written in 1491 to a friend is entitled 'On the four kinds of divine frenzy and the praises of Lorenzo de' Medici'. It begins: 'In our time we have known a most blessed spirit...'[13] A portrait of Lorenzo in one illuminated manuscript of this period (Biblioteque Nationale, Paris) reveals his fine ascetic features and expresses that quality of inner peace and serenity which he now enjoyed. Lorenzo's death in 1492 was accompanied by storms, natural catastrophes and omens, which Ficino said, follow on the death of great heroes.

To return to Ficino; in keeping with his wish to bring philosophy and religion together Ficino took holy orders in 1473 and wrote a work on the Christian religion. Later Ficino was made a Canon of Florence Cathedral through Medici generosity and Lorenzo even tried, though unsuccessfully, to obtain a bishopric for Ficino. Although many of his friends were churchmen and he was very influential in ecclesiastical circles, throughout his life Ficino faced opposition and censure from the church on account of his Platonic teachings. This increased dramatically following his publication of *The Three Books of Life*. Another episode may account for this.

In the early 1480s a brilliant scholar, Pico della Mirandola, came to Florence, gifted with exceptional talent for speech and debate, a prodigy even by the standards of that age. Attracted to Ficino and the Academy he made such rapid progress in his studies that he soon conceived the idea of harmonising all systems of religious and philosophical thought in a universal synthesis. In 1486 in preparation for this he published nine hundred articles in theology, philosophy, logic and other subjects which he declared himself ready to defend in public debate. Some of these articles were extremely radical and seemed like a challenge to the dogmas of the Catholic faith. Pico proposed the forum for this public debate should be Rome, heartland of the church and he offered to refund the travelling expenses of anyone wishing to attend to attract as many participants as possible. The Pope then in office was Innocent VIII; although he was mild-natured, moderate in his views, and on friendly terms with Lorenzo de Medici, these articles aroused maximum consternation in Rome, and at the eleventh hour the proposed debate was banned. Pico was requested to attend a commission of enquiry. Some of the articles were declared heretical and Pico was forbidden from debating these issues any further. But he published an apology in which he sought to explain and justify the condemned articles. The *Apology* was actually published clandestinely in a pamphlet probably by radical student friends of Pico's. The authorities were incensed. Pico was outlawed and he fled to France and the protection of the Dauphin where he was briefly imprisoned for his own safety. Lorenzo de' Medici and other friends intervened on his behalf and he was allowed to return to Italy.

Ficino had encouraged Pico from the start, and he now urged Pico to return to Florence, which he did. Pico spent the next six years until his death in 1494 writing philosophical and theological works, in spite of facing continuing hostility from the church. An eloquent testimony of the encouragement and support Pico received from Ficino throughout this period is contained in their letters. When Pico died Ficino wrote these words to a mutual friend of theirs: 'As a young man Pico was like a son to me; in friendship he was a brother to me; in love he was my very self.'[14]

Whilst Pico's fate demonstrated the dangers in speaking out openly and boldly challenging the church's authority at this time, Ficino's manner of approach was very different, but because of his connection with Pico the authorities in Rome turned their attention to his writings.

Also as the century drew to a close, the church was becoming increasingly intolerant of any opposition to her teachings; even during the Pontificate of Innocent VIII the inquisition was given new power to combat heresy and witchcraft, and the first papal Bull aimed at controlling the printing of books containing false and erroneous material was enacted (1487). In 1489 Ficino chose to publish a seminal work on medicine, the 'three books of life', *De Vita Libri Tres*, concerned with the total health of man. Ficino had already published a translation of Plato's *Dialogues* with commentaries, including the *Symposium* commentary on love, and a major work, *Platonic Theology*, on the immortality of souls. Ficino's work on *The Christian Religion* had, it seems, faced some scrutiny when first published in 1476. Members of the church who believed Ficino was spreading ideas incompatible with orthodox dogma made false allegations against him; Ficino appealed to his friends, including three lawyers, one ambassador and the Archbishop of Florence, Rinaldo Orsini, to exert all their influence with the Pope in this matter, and at the eleventh hour the authorities were persuaded to drop their investigations. The Dominicans, who could establish a Commission to examine suspect writings, may have been involved. This order, dubbed *Domino canes*, hounds of the Lord, had earned a fearsome reputation as guardians of orthodoxy, but the Italian order was milder than its Spanish or German counterparts. Ficino playfully refers to three friends who defended him as hounds of the Academy and his critics and opponents as wolves, bats and night creatures, *vespertiliones*. Of course Ficino would have argued convincingly, and persuaded his critics with love, that his teachings and writings were in complete accord with Christianity. Details of the accusations are not known, but from his correspondence we may infer that the authorities focused on such topics as magic, astrology and astral influences; that the heavenly bodies are living creatures. Facing mounting opposition from its critics, the Platonic Academy disguised its identity and effectively went underground, whilst continuing to enjoy Medici protection.

Towards the close of the fifteenth century, a backlash against the entire cultural movement of the Renaissance was threatened; a reaction which sought to undermine all the work of unity and healing which had proceeded for more than a century.

The Dominican monk Girolamo Savonarola was in the vanguard of this reactionary movement. Invited to Florence on the recommendation of Pico della Mirandola it seems, he tried to reform the church and society largely by a return to the ideals and values of the Middle Ages; he preached mainly to the people in sermons characterised by a fierce denunciation of vice and corruption and the wickedness of men, especially those placed in authority, and the swift retribution which would fall on their heads. He sought to separate religion from philosophy, and faith from reason. Instead of healing division within society he created further divisions; political factions multiplied; some supported his reforms whilst others opposed them.

After the expulsion of the Medici from Florence in 1494, Savonarola presented himself as the prophet of a new Christian republic. His radical ideas gained more support and bonfires of vanities, including paintings and books, were staged. His influence extended to all levels of society including artists and craftsmen. Botticelli and Lorenzo di Credi were among those moved by his sermons. Some of Ficino's closest friends fell under his spell. Pico della Mirandola tried to moderate Savonarola's radicalism, but after Pico's death the Dominican friar grew even more extreme in his rejection of philosophy and secular culture. He openly denounced the Borgia Pope Alexander VI and the Catholic hierarchy. The Pope ordered him to desist from preaching under threat of excommunication. When he defied this ban he was condemned and burnt at the stake in dramatic circumstances. Florence was deeply divided over the issue and Savonarola's partisans kept his memory alive long after his death.

At the start Ficino expressed his faith in Savonarola and even defended him on one occasion, but became increasingly disillusioned with Savonarola's hysterical rhetoric and distanced himself from the friar, advising others to do likewise. Indeed Ficino had once given these words of advice to an orator and his pupils: 'let them censure the fault which is the act of a friend, not blame the man, which is the act of an enemy.'[15] After Savonarola's death Ficino wrote an *Apology* on behalf of the people of Florence who, he said, had been greatly deceived by this arch-hypocrite.[16]

We have hardly touched on the Academy which in its heyday included some of the most brilliant minds of the century. In one letter Ficino does list some forty of its most distinguished members. Contemporary writers, however make little mention of the Academy; which has prompted some scholars to question its very existence. But members were sworn to secrecy and discretion, not to speak with impunity of the work of the Academy outside its walls, especially during the last years of Lorenzo's rule. Ficino's letters do mention the Academy but they were only published in 1495 when the Medici were no longer in Florence. By then the main work of the Academy had been accomplished and everything could be viewed in retrospect as history.

The culmination of the work of the Academy is best summarised by Ficino in his letter to Paul of Middleberg in which he describes the rebirth of the liberal arts and the restoration of the Platonic teachings, including the art of singing to the Orphic lyre, all of which he said had taken place in Florence. Never attributing its achievements to himself, Ficino expresses gratitude for the grace of God in allowing a touch of the Golden Age to manifest at a time of increasing uncertainty.[17]

The life of the Academy did not end with Ficino's death in 1499; it lived on in the new academies of the sixteenth and seventeenth centuries devoted to the arts and sciences.

Ficino designated Francesco Cattani da Diaccetto to take his place as head of the Academy. Members now included artists. This Academy was associated with another group that met in the gardens of the Rucellai villa under Bernardo Rucellai, and which included Macchiavelli.

Some of the greatest minds of the Renaissance belonged to an academy; from Alberti to Leonardo da Vinci, who wanted to establish his own academy in Milan. This also applies to the later academies; Galileo Galilei belonged to the Academy of the Lincei, the 'lynx-eyed ones'; Sir Isaac Newton belonged to the Royal Society; and these later academies regarded themselves as sharing in the same tradition as the

Renaissance Academy that had first flourished in the time of Cosimo de' Medici.

Whilst the later academies tended to specialise in one or more branches of human knowledge, the earlier academies, as Dame Frances Yates has observed, were informal groups whose 'marvellous intellectual vitality seems to embrace the whole range of human activity.'[18]

But the real spirit of Ficino's Academy is well summed up in the closing lines of Ficino's Life of Plato: 'For our part let us venerate Plato's life and wisdom, in the judgement of the wise regarded as the best, and together with Apuleius of Madaura let us freely proclaim: "we, the family of Plato, know nothing except what is bright, joyful, celestial and supreme".'[19]

NOTES

1. *The Letters of Marsilio Ficino*, Shepheard-Walwyn, Vol. 4, letter no. 11. (Subsequently cited as *Letters*.)
2. Marsyas the Satire: see Plato *Symposium*, 215.
3. *Letters*, 1, 107.
4. *Letters*, 4, 12.
5. *Proem* to the first ten Platonic dialogues translated by Ficino; see P.O. Kristeller, *Supplementum Ficinianum*, Florence 1937, Vol.2, pp. 103-4.
6. Description of Cosimo's last hours, in Ficino's preface to Xenocrates, *De Morte*, Marsilius Ficinus, *Opera Omnia* II p. 1965. (Basle 1576; reprint. Turin 1959.)
7. Ficinus, *Opera* p. 1129
8. *Letters*, 1, 26.
9. See *Marsilio Ficino: The Philebus Commentary*, ed. Michael J.B. Allen. (Appendix III p. 482.)
10. See Nesca A. Robb, *Neoplatonism of the Italian Renaissance*, p. 165, and appendix p. 291.
11. For an account of the Pazzi Conspiracy see *Letters* 4, pp. 73-91; and *Letters* 5, pp. 85-91.
12. *Letters*, 5, pp. 3-8; pp. 15-19; pp. 23-30.
13. Ficinus, *Opera*, p. 927.
14. *Supplementum*, Vol. 2, pp. 91-92 (letter to Germain de Ganay).

15. *Letters*, 1, 109.
16. See *Supplementum*, Vol. 2, pp. 76-79.
17. Ficinus, *Opera*, p. 944.
18. Frances A. Yates, 'The Italian Academies' p. 7 (in Frances A. Yates, *Renaissance and Reform: The Italian Contribution*) London, 1983.
19. *Letters*, 3, p. 48

A Man of Compassion

CLEMENT SALAMAN

Nothing displeases God more than to be ignored.
Nothing pleases Him more than to be adored. *

TO ME Ficino's most attractive quality is his compassionate tolerance. I well remember when I first went up to Oxford as a young man, being approached by various so-called Christian organisations with a view to making me join one of their groups. Admirable as they seemed in so many ways, what put me off was their total conviction that theirs was the only way to salvation. They reminded me of the cartoon of a company of soldiers marching. Two women are watching them. One turns to the other and says: 'Look! My Johnny is the only one in step!' How different in spirit from Ficino's *Christian Religion* where he writes 'It is of more concern to the greatest king that he be honoured sincerely rather than by one kind of ritual or another... He prefers to be worshipped in any way, even unfittingly, if it is proper to man, rather than not to be worshipped at all through pride.'[1]

Marsilio's whole life was an expression of unity, for he never ceased in his attempts to bring people together as one. In the Italy in which he lived, revenge demanded by honour was a significant part of the culture, so magnificently captured by Shakespeare in *Romeo and Juliet*. The earlier law of 'An eye for an eye and a tooth for a tooth' was never quite covered, even by a thick veneer of the Christian religion. Quite a number of Ficino's letters are urging patience and tolerance upon the recipients. To his 'unique' friend Giovanni Cavalcanti he writes: 'Have you not seen puppies snapping at a stone that has been thrown at

* Ficino, *De Christiana Religione*

29

them, even though it has not hit them? Although they have not been hurt by the stone they hurt their teeth when they bite it... You will perhaps say that it is difficult not to desire vengeance. But be in no doubt that if men forgive, the most just God will settle the balance a little later. What could be easier, what more glorious than reliance on God as one's avenger, and to learn as much goodness from Him by patience as the wicked meant to inflict injury, and thus to transform evil into good'.[2]

Ficino's efforts to bring his friends and correspondents into harmony were unremitting. But he also understood that if people persist in inflicting harm, then only by suffering will they come to understand that to harm others is to harm oneself. That is what he means when he says of the puppies that although the stones thrown by other people did not hurt them, they hurt their teeth when they bite them. How close he was, not only to the academy of Plato but also to the spirit of the Greek tragedy! At the end of Sophocles' Antigone the anti-hero Creon had to endure the suicides of his wife and son because of his ruthless desire for vengeance which he now bitterly regrets. The Chorus comment in the final lines of the play that in the end the blows of fate 'will teach us wisdom' (in other words we shall learn by suffering). That is what Ficino means when he says, 'the most just God will settle the balance a little later'. In countless ingenious ways Ficino explains to a host of his correspondents that in reality he and his correspondent are one, and that other members of the Academy, with whom he is also one, send their greetings. He writes to Francesco Bandini that he must have eyes like a lynx because he has immediately seen what it took Ficino ten years to discover and five years to write about: that although he and Cavalcanti have separate bodies, there is but one within.[3]

Ficino's correspondence to leading citizens of many states was vast, filling twelve books of letters and ranging over many countries. No wonder that he was able to remark (perhaps half humorously) towards the end of his life that 'he held all Europe in loving servitude.'[4] Ficino was no ivory tower philosopher, enclosing himself in his academy of friends while Europe went to rack and ruin. His outstanding literary and philosophical achievements were his translations and commentaries on the works of Plato and the neo-platonists. Nevertheless he followed Plato's practice in Syracuse rather than his principles in the *Republic*. In other words, when the times required he participated in state affairs, even though Socrates excuses a philosopher from this in an imperfect state. It is true that his participation was behind the scenes, but for all that, unmistakable. In 1478 the Pazzi Conspiracy ended up with the assassination of Giuliano de' Medici in Florence Cathedral; and Lorenzo his brother, the ruler of Florence, was very nearly killed as well. Ficino was on close terms with two of the conspirators: Jacopo Bracciolini and Francesco Salviati, Archbishop of Pisa. It is extremely unlikely that Ficino knew anything of their precise plans, but he sensed that their attitude was dangerous to the State and urged them as strongly as possible not to go down the path of treason.[5]

His letters to Pope Sixtus IV show how he not only worked for peace and harmony within the State but also within the Church and between states. The Pope had been heavily involved in the Pazzi Conspiracy. For he saw Lorenzo as the main obstacle to his territorial ambitions in Northern Italy and also to his desire for getting a tighter control over the church in Florence. When his attempt to have Lorenzo murdered failed, he declared war on Florence in alliance with King Ferrante of Naples and placed Florence under interdict (forbidding all church services). Florence was saved by the courageous action of Lorenzo in visiting unannounced the Court of Ferrante and persuading him to withdraw his army; and secondly by the landing of the Turks in Southern Italy which meant that the Pope too had to withdraw his army.

But Ficino's letters,[6] whether or not they ever reached the Pope, stand as masterpieces. On first reading, the longer letters strike one as sublime irony rivalling that of Gibbon or Pascal, for they praise the Pope for the very qualities he is most conspicuously not showing. For the attack on Florence was as cruel as it was unjust. Ficino writes *Letters*, 5.9 on Christmas Day 1478: 'Our Sixtus, conspicuous for his piety, a father in the tradition of the holy fathers, kisses his children all the more sweetly after his fatherly threats and rebukes, kindly takes them to his breast and enfolds them with his loving arms. And as he mistakenly seemed a little while ago to be pursuing his children with malice, so undoubtedly is he soon to attend them with love. Now, everyone, hear! Hear the gracious voice of our shepherd. Look more closely at his joyful countenance which brings all things to peace by its blessing. Surely you see it? Even now he is opening his mouth to cry out to his flock, with his Lord: Peace be with you, my children, in the new year. Be not afraid: I am no wolf but a guardian, no hireling but a shepherd, the shepherd sent into the world by Him through whom the world was made, who both was in the world and was sent into the world, not to lose his sheep but to save them and to lay down his life for them.'

Although the above is a short extract from a fairly long letter it is a good example of the ironical praise that Ficino bestows upon Sixtus IV. However, looked at from another viewpoint this letters holds up to Sixtus a kind of mirror in which, if he chose, he could see what a true pope would have been, what he himself could be, what his inner nature really was. Ficino writes as if he could actually see the Pope's actions coming into line with the nature of his office. 'Look more closely at his joyful countenance which brings all things to peace by its blessing. Surely you see it?' Such words affect the mental environment in which men think and in which events happen.

At the deeper cultural level Ficino worked to fuse the traditions of philosophy and religion. The religious foundation of Europe was the Mosaic law interpreted by the Hebrew prophets and transformed by Christ's doctrine of love into burning faith; a faith which led to the revelation of God through devotion. The philosophic tradition sprang from teachings of Pythagoras systematised by Plato and Aristotle and fully expounded by a series of later philosophers, of whom the greatest was Plotinus. Fundamentally their goal was knowledge of truth and their tool was reason. Even in the twelth century the religious and philosophic traditions had never quite met, and since that century they had grown further apart. The view of the theologians throughout the Middle Ages was that knowledge was obtained mainly through divine revelation. William of Ockham claimed that knowledge arose only through divine revelation. Philosophy was left in a very inferior position.

Around the year 1462 Cosimo de' Medici, Ficino's patron and ruler of Florence from 1434 to 1464 acquired a Greek manuscript of a previously lost work: the *Corpus Hermeticum* (then known as the *Poimandres*, the title of the first book). Cosimo was both a great lover of Plato and a deeply devout Christian who had no doubt been troubled by the apparent irreconcilability of Plato and Christ. Even before the newly discovered work was formally translated, Cosimo may have divined that the work contained the seeds of a resolution to the difficulty. In 1462 Ficino had been commissioned by Cosimo to translate all the works of Plato. However, hardly had he got started on this work when Cosimo asked him to suspend the translations until he had rendered the *Corpus Hermeticum* into Latin. In his introduction to this work, dedicated to Cosimo, Ficino (drawing on St Augustine's *City of God*) states that: 'At the time when Moses was born, there flourished Atlas the astrologer, brother of the physician Prometheus and maternal grandfather of the Greater Hermes, whose grandson was Hermes Trismegistus.' The Egyptians, he said, 'declare that Trismegistus was truly thrice greatest, because he stood out as the greatest philosopher, the greatest priest and the greatest king.' Ficino goes on to say that the Egyptian kings were also priests. He did not need to remind his readers that Moses was brought up as the son of a Pharaoh and therefore would have had access to the same priestly wisdom, which did not change over the centuries.

Ficino may even have credited the words of Artapanus, a second century BC Jewish writer quoted in Eusebius, 'For these reasons then Moses was beloved by the multitudes and being deemed by the priests worthy to be honoured like a god, was named Hermes because of his interpretation of the hieroglyphics'.[7] In other words Hermes Trismegistus and Moses were one and the same person!

Ficino certainly accepted the statement of Artapanus recorded by Eusebius in the same chapter in his *Preparation for the Gospel* where Artapanus declares: 'This Moses, they said, was the teacher of Orpheus.' Presumably on the strength of these quotations from

Eusebius, Ficino writes in his Preface to his translation of 'the book of Hermes Trismegistus addressed to Cosimo de' Medici: 'Hermes is called the first father of theology. Aglaophemus was initiated into the sacred mysteries by Orpheus, to be succeeded in theology by Pythagoras who in turn was followed by Philolaus, the teacher of our divine Plato.'

The publication of Ficino's translation and commentary in 1471 was enormously influential in dissolving the' dichotomy between the Greek philosophic tradition and Christianity. The most obvious and eloquent testimony to this is the floor of Siena Cathedral where the large figure of Hermes Trismegistus appears on the pavement close to the West door appearing to give his teaching to auditors both from East and West. Here Hermes is described as 'Contemporary of Moses'. This pavement was laid down in the 1480s. So greatly was the authority of the classical philosophers strengthened that Ficino was able to write (1474-5) to Bernardo Bembo within three to four years of the publication of his translation 'Lawful philosophy is no different from true religion, and lawful religion exactly the same as true philosophy.'[8] The fusing of these two strands in Western culture was of great significance in determining the direction the Renaissance was to take.[9]

The motive force behind Ficino's desire for harmony and reconciliation was Love. Beauty and Love were the centre of his system. As he explains in his commentary on Plato's *Symposium*: 'This Divine Beauty creates in everything love, that is, desire for itself; because if God draws the world to Himself, and the World is drawn from Him there is one continuous attraction, beginning with God, going to the World, and ending at last in God, an attraction which returns to the same place whence it began as though in a kind of circle.'[10]

Ultimately this beauty is the beauty of the One which is within everything and comprehends the apparent multiplicity. 'The soul sleeps in the prison of the material body but when it sees reflections or hears resonances of that divine beauty in the physical realm it begins to yearn for that beauty with unutterable ardour. It then begins to grow wings with which it may fly back to its divine homeland.'[11]

The presentation of beauty in all forms of art and literature therefore had a profoundly spiritual purpose, which was to draw the beholders to that realm where there could no disagreement, no disharmony. It was no accident that Ficino lists among members of his academy the architect Alberti, and that he was on close terms with the painter Antonio Pollaiuolo.[12] Nor is it surprising that Botticelli, with whom Ficino must have been in frequent contact within the Medici Circle, painted such pictures as the *Primavera* and the *Birth of Venus*, pictures of exquisite beauty and containing profound Platonic meaning.

Ficino lived as he taught, a life devoted to reconciliation and unity. His contemporary biographer Giovanni Corsi[13] describes him walking round Florence, like Socrates, attracting the young people to him by the power of his words; and how their mutual love grew. He used his considerable medical knowledge on his very a wide circle of friends free of charge. He also gave the whole of his share of his father's inheritance to be divided up between his brothers. Meanwhile like Socrates he lived with very few possessions and was abstemious over food. While very much in the world he was untouched by it.

NOTES

1. *De Christiana Religione*, Cap.4
2. *The Letters of Marsilio Ficino*, 1, letter 49, Shepheard-Walwyn, London.
3. *Ibid.* 1.111
4. *Opera*, p.891
5. See correspondence to Bracciolini and Salviati in *Letters*, *passim*, especially 3.36
6. See especially *Letters* 5.1. & 5.9
7. Eusebius, *Preparation for the Gospel*, Book IX, Cap.XXVII
8. *Letters*, 1.7
9. One might cite especially here the field of education. Many features of English Public School education, at least up to 40 years ago, carried strong resonances of Plato's education for the Guardians outlined in his *Republic*. For correspondence between Ficino and John Colet see *John Colet and Marsilio Ficino*, Sears Jayne, OUP, 1963. Colet was the founder of the new St Paul's School in London

10. *De Amore*, Orato 2, Cap.2
11. *Letters*, 1.7
12. *Letters*, 6.26
13. 'Life of Marsilio Ficino' by Giovanni Corsi, *Letters,* Vol.3

In Praise of the One –
Marsilio Ficino and *Advaita*

ARTHUR FARNDELL

*God is unchanging unity; a single stillness**

A Little About Advaita

Advaita is a simple and most profound philosophy. It is known as
the philosophy of unity, for it affirms a single reality. Although this
reality is beyond words, being itself the source of all words, the human
desire to express the inexpressible furnishes a plethora of descriptions.
Some of these, acknowledging the impossibility of the task they are
attempting, are couched in apparently negative terms. Thus the one
reality is presented as unknowable, unthinkable, and immeasurable.
Other accounts are buoyantly positive and describe reality as truth,
consciousness, bliss, and love.

A Little about Ficino

Marsilio Ficino is a simple and most profound philosopher. Indeed,
we may apply to him the words with which he addressed Pietro Leone:
*vir omnium integerrime, imo et omnium simplicissime*ᵃ – 'a man more
wholly himself than all others and, in fact, simpler than all others.'
His words transmit truth, consciousness, bliss, and love; and under
his guidance people are led from the darkness of ignorance to the light
of knowledge.

Ficino's Definition of God

In the words which Ficino puts into the mouth of Dionysius we

---

* Ficino, *Letters*, Vol 1, letter 11

37

find a negation to end all negations, but even this supreme negation eventually switches to a positive mode. This is how Ficino's imaginary dialogue with Dionysius on the nature of the Trinity comes to an end:

'God is not soul; God does not have sense, or imagination, opinion, reason, or intelligence. God is not intellect, not intelligence. God is neither spoken nor understood. God is not number, not order, not greatness, not smallness, not equality, not similarity, not dissimilarity. God does not stay, does not move, does not seek rest. He does not have power, nor is He power or light, life or essence, eternity or time, intelligible self-awareness or knowledge. Indeed, He is not truth, not dominion, not wisdom, not one, not unity, not goodness, not deity ... Nor is He any of those things that are not or of those that are... God has no speech, no name, no consciousness, no shadows, no light, no untruth, no truth. He has no position, no lack of position. In truth, we are the ones who position or remove those things which are secondary to God, but Him we do not position, and Him we do not remove, for being above all position He is the totally perfect cause of all things, and being beyond all possibility of removal He is the perfection of the one who is absolutely detached from everything and higher than all.'[b]

God Fills The Universe

Ficino is an ardent apostle of the *summum bonum,* one of the positive names of the single reality. The maxim around the walls of his Academy began: 'All things are directed from goodness to goodness.'[1] The necessary corollary of a single reality that is wholly good is that evil has no real existence. Ficino makes his position very clear: 'We know that the one ruler of the whole universe, who directs and moves such a great body so well over so great a span of time without ever wearying, is good and without limit. If He is indisputably without limit and reproduces Himself infinitely throughout space and surpasses everything infinitely in degree of virtue, where then does evil dwell, if it cannot exist with the good, and the good itself fills the universe? Evil therefore has no true place anywhere, only an imaginary one.'[2]

The Universe is a Reflection of The Absolute

The philosophy of unity causes all of Ficino's affirmations about the One to be equally incisive and uncompromising. In a note to Giovanni Cavalcanti, written by Ficino in 1476 to accompany the preface to one of his theological works, he reminds Giovanni that 'God cannot be moved anywhere, since for Him there is no external space, for He completely fills everything from the inside and totally encompasses everything from the outside.'[3] In an earlier letter to Cavalcanti, Ficino expresses the quintessentially *advaitic* view by declaring that the universe itself is but a reflection of the Absolute: 'Are we right to say that there is one world? Would it not be more correct to say that there are many, or indeed innumerable worlds? In truth there is one, since it is formed in the image of one…So that this world should be most like that Absolute Being in its unity, neither two nor an infinite number of worlds were created, but one only-begotten world has ever been, and ever will be.'[4]

Some Influences Upon Ficino

How did Ficino become an unequivocal exponent of the philosophy of unity? It happened, in large measure, through his contact with the writings of earlier exponents, for his translations included the *Hymns* of Orpheus, the *Sayings* of Zoroaster, and the works of Hermes Trismegistus. Yet it is not to these venerable figures that Ficino constantly alludes, but to Plato. The work of translating into Latin the collected writings of Plato and composing his own commentaries on the Socratic dialogues made an indelible impression on Ficino's consciousness. One effect can be seen in the twelve books of Ficino's letters, which contain nearly 900 references, direct and indirect, to Plato. Ficino never tires of calling him *Plato noster* and, on occasions, *divinus Plato* or *divus Plato*. Ficino's writings are full of quotations from Plato and paraphrases of passages in the *Dialogues*. The words that close our previous paragraph, for example, are a very faithful reflection of what *Timaeus* says. Ficino goes so far as to declare that

Plato's main purpose was to advocate the philosophy of unity: 'It was the chief work of the divine Plato, as the dialogues of *Parmenides* and *Epinomis* show, to reveal the principle of unity in all things, which he called appropriately the One itself. He also asserted that in all things there is one truth, that is, the light of the One itself, the light of God, which is poured into all minds and forms, presenting the forms to the minds and joining the minds to the forms.'[5] Ficino also tells us that 'Every day he [Plato] used to repeat, "The eternal alone is true, the temporal only seems to be." '[6]

Advaita in the 'Platonic Theology'

Ficino saw his own work as parallel to that of Plato, and he laboured long to show that Christianity and the Platonic teaching are essentially identical. The fruits of his labours are preserved in the eighteen books of his *Platonic Theology*, comprising some quarter of a million words. In the preface to his *magnum opus*, which is dedicated to Lorenzo de' Medici, Ficino refers to the original impulse that gave rise to this imposing edifice, which rests upon sound foundations and is designed by the sure eye and hand of a master architect: 'Relying on St Augustine's authority and prompted by supreme love for mankind, I decided long ago to portray Plato's own likeness in its close resemblance to the Christian truth'[c] The first chapter of the second book concludes with a simple *advaitic* statement: 'For these reasons, the unity and truth and goodness which we find above the angels, according to the mind of Plato, is the source of all, the one God, true and good.'[d] The following chapter contains elegant and cogent arguments against duality and plurality, and chapter three of the second book presents closely argued reasons for not accepting plurality and ends with these beautiful words about God: 'Because He is unity, He is also truth, and because He is true unity, He is also goodness. In unity He enfolds all, in truth He unfolds all, and through goodness He pours forth all. But when all has flowed forth from Him, it flows back through goodness, is reformed through truth, and is restored to one through unity.'[e]

Advaita a Living Reality

Although the *Platonic Theology* is a masterpiece of close-knit reasoning and a valid demonstration of the one truth proclaimed in the Christian Scriptures and in the Platonic dialogues, it is important to remember that in Ficino's life the philosophy of unity is a living reality and not a series of logical postulates. It is in his letters that Ficino demonstrates this practical reality most directly. Writing to Cosimo de' Medici, who himself had visualised and implemented the spread of Platonic teaching by gathering all of Plato's extant writings and arranging for Ficino to translate them all into Latin, he says: 'Since therefore we all wish to be happy, and happiness cannot be obtained without the right use of our gifts, and since knowledge reveals their proper use, we should leave all else aside and strive with the full support of philosophy and religion to become as wise as possible. For thus our soul becomes most like to God, who is wisdom itself.'[7] To Gregorio Epifanio, priest and philosopher, Ficino says, 'Let us, my Gregorio, retire into that one unmoving watch-tower of the mind, where, as Plato says, the unseen light will shine unceasingly upon us.'[8]

Advaita and Purification

Ficino recognises that human beings need to live a life of unity, and he tells Francesco Lapaccini and Migliore Cresci the most direct way to achieve this: 'Those men seek God the most direct way who first of all cut back the immoderate desires of the soul through the civil virtues. They then cut them back to the quick by the purgatorial virtues. Thus cleansed, in the third stage they root them out with all their might through the virtues that belong to the purified soul. When these desires have been rooted out, as far as is humanly possible, such men finally are formed by the model virtues which are in God.'[9] Freedom from bodily taint, Ficino tells Giovanni Cavalcanti, 'we gain principally through the three virtues of prudence, justice and piety. Prudence recognises what we owe to God and what to the world. Justice gives its due to the world, and piety its due to God. Thus the man of prudence yields his body, as a limb of the world, to the turmoil of the world wherever it happens to move it. But his soul, the offspring of

God, he removes from all dealings with the body and freely commits to the guidance of divine providence.'[10]

Steps Towards Advaita

It is also in his letters that Ficino is happy to offer step-by-step practices that can be implemented by anyone willing to follow them. He weaves his instructions into a running narrative so that they are scarcely noticed. Here, extracted from its context, is one practice which he advocates: 'Do you desire to look on the face of good? Then look around at the whole universe, full of the light of the sun. Look at the light in the material world, full of all forms in constant movement; take away the matter, leave the rest. You have the soul, an incorporeal light that takes all shapes and is full of change. Once again, take from this the changeability, and now you have reached the intelligence of the angels, the incorporeal light, taking all shapes but unchanging. Take away from this that diversity by which any form differs from the light, and which is infused into the light from elsewhere, and then the essence of the light and of each form is the same; the light gives form to itself and through its own forms gives form to everything.'[11]

Advaita and Love

The steps towards appreciating the single reality necessarily open the heart as well as the intellect, and Ficino's writings are alive with love for God, love for truth, love for goodness, love for beauty, love for all mankind; love which yearns for everyone to come to the simple realisation which graced his own life and which is expressed in two chapter headings of his magnificent commentary to Plato's *Symposium.* The first is 'Love is within all and throughout all, caring for all and instructing all.'[f] The second is 'Love is the creator of all and the preserver of all.'[g] The best way, however, to conclude the current essay on Marsilio Ficino and *advaita* is to quote the words of the Psalmist which Ficino himself was fond of repeating: 'Behold how good, and how pleasant it is, for brethren to dwell together in unity.'[12]

NOTES

The quotations denoted by Arabic numerals are from translations published by Shepheard-Walwyn under the title *The Letters of Marsilio Ficino*. Quotations denoted by lower-case letters are translated by the author of this article from the Bottega d'Erasmo 1962 facsimile reprint of the 1576 Basel Edition of Ficino's *Opera Omnia*.

1. Vol. 1, p.40
2. Vol. 4, p.47
3. Vol. 2, p.34
4. Vol. 1, p.87
5. Vol. 1, p.84
6. Vol. 3, p.44
7. Vol. 1, p34
8. Vol. 1, p.51
9. Vol. 1, pp.57,58
10. Vol. 1, p.95
11. Vol. 1, pp.37,38
12. Vol. 4, p.57

a. p.928
b. p.1024
c. p.78
d. p.93
e. p.96
f. p.1328
g. p.1329

Fellow Philosophers

LINDA PROUD

Friendship between men cannot be kindled
unless God breathes upon it*

IN the literary tradition of collected letters, it is not unusual for the correspondence to be one-sided; after all, we do not know what the Colossians and Corinthians wrote to St Paul before he wrote back to them. The translators of Ficino's letters have tried to make good this deficiency by including in each volume short biographies of the correspondents, but this book celebrating Ficino's quincentenary provides an opportunity to invite two of his friends to step out from their 'brief lives' in the appendix, and to give us a glimpse of Ficino through eyes other than our own.

The romantic view of the Platonic Academy is that of a group of men gathered round the Medici hearth, or in the shade of a loggia, reading Plato. Always such pictures will include Angelo Poliziano, the poet, and Giovanni Pico della Mirandola, the philosopher. Without doubt there was such a group, and it did include these men, centred on the powerful figure of Lorenzo de' Medici himself, but their discussions were much more challenging and contentious than our imaginations would have us suppose.

Our story begins in 1479, a low year in the fortunes of the Medici family. The year before Lorenzo's younger brother Giuliano had died in a murderous attack on the Medici that had been planned in the Vatican. Afterwards, the Pope excommunicated Lorenzo on the grounds that he was the cause rather than the victim of the trouble – a bold

---

* Ficino, *Letters*, Vol 3, letter 31

44

accusation even in those days. The Pope commanded the Florentines to give up their Lorenzo to justice, but the city preferred to share Lorenzo's excommunication, even though it meant war with Rome and her ally Naples. The war lasted until 1480. In that time, while the enemy forces destroyed the crops and farms of Tuscany, and Florence fell victim to plague, famine and flood, Lorenzo's family were hidden in the country under the care of his friend, the poet Angelo Poliziano, but Ficino remained in his villa on Careggi busy completing his translation of Plato's dialogues.

Travel, never easy, must have been particularly difficult in those days, and yet it is in 1479 that we hear of a sixteen year old student of philosophy and theology arriving in the city. That Giovanni Pico della Mirandola met Angelo Poliziano and Ficino, we know for certain, and it is probable that he also met Lorenzo de' Medici. We are told by several writers that, as well as being brilliant, Pico was a beautiful young man, grave, thoughtful and noble, but our Florentines may well have dismissed him as one more prodigious youth, a passing comet demanding but their brief attention in these darkest of days, when each of them faced a personal crisis. Lorenzo, fighting for the life of his family and city, was also contending against the demons of self-doubt. Ficino, suspected of being part of the conspiracy, was under official investigation. As for Poliziano, he was locked in terrible combat with Lorenzo de' Medici's wife.

He, the foremost poet of his age, fluent in Latin and Greek, of superb intellect and with a profound sensitivity for language, had been given the task of educating Lorenzo's eldest son. This was no simple appointment as a tutor, but a role of the highest importance, one quite probably steered by Ficino, since Lorenzo's son was to be raised as the 'philosopher-king' on the Platonic model. But Clarice, alone with him in the country, and outside the range of her husband's authority, took it upon herself to alter the reading matter of the boys from Plato and Cicero to Christian scripture. Though this may be enough in itself to explain the furore, we may infer other, deeper causes for Clarice to attack Lorenzo's friend and throw him out of the house. Distressed by Lorenzo's excommunication from the Church she so loved, wounded by her husband's infidelity, pregnant for the ninth time, she was angry and afraid. Did she believe that everything happening was divine retribution for her husband's sin? If so, she took it out *on his philosophy* in the person of the tutor. After all, Poliziano was standing *in loco parentis*, but without the power and authority naturally held by husband and father, and therefore she could deal with him in a way she could not deal with Lorenzo. Poliziano took the brunt of Clarice's wrath, lost his place in the household, but retained Lorenzo's love.

When Poliziano returned to Florence after the expulsion, Lorenzo housed him in his villa on Fiesole, and there he spent the summer relieved of all duties, free to study and write. Thus two great minds – Ficino's and Poliziano's – were freed from concern at a time when Lorenzo himself was battling to save his house and city from destruction. Such was the magnanimity of the Magnificent. But this leisure was to have short duration: towards the end of Advent, Lorenzo was impelled to sail to Naples to negotiate in person with the enemy, a mission planned in secret and fraught with danger. Poliziano had been told to prepare himself for the journey, but for some reason – presumably the ill-willed intervention of another – Lorenzo left without him; humiliated, Poliziano left his beloved Florence and went north to look for a new patron.

It must have been sometime during those summer months on Fiesole that the first meeting took place of those men destined to become companions of the soul: Ficino, Pico and Poliziano. After this first meeting, Pico wrote to Ficino and asked for a copy of his *Platonic Theology*; from Poliziano he wanted a copy of the *Manual of Epictetus* that Poliziano was translating from Greek. But the friendship, which was to prove so enduring, and was to end with Pico and Poliziano sharing the same tomb, did not properly begin until 1484, by which time Pico had shown that he was no mere shooting star of precocity.

Giovanni Pico della Mirandola

In that year, Ficino completed his life's work, the translation of Plato from Greek into Latin. Where lesser mortals might scrabble to find some other task to occupy themselves, Ficino seems to have waited for divine instruction. He did not have to wait long: the answer came on the heels of the completion, and was indeed the result of a divine, not to say *Cosmic* (to use a Ficinian pun) intervention. The messenger was Giovanni Pico, by now twenty-one years old and the Count of Concordia. Ficino tells us the story himself in his preface to his translation of Plotinus. It begins with an account of how the great Cosimo de' Medici – Lorenzo's grandfather had been inspired to found the Platonic Academy, how he had destined Ficino for the task, provided him with all the Greek works of Plato and Plotinus, and entrusted him with the translation of Hermes Trismegistus and Plato. 'I completed Hermes in a few months, whilst Cosimo was still living. If he had wanted me to do Plotinus also, he made no mention of it, lest he should burden me with too heavy a load. Such was his clemency and modesty towards everyone. Thus I did not undertake Plotinus, though I would not have refused it.' Having completed the Plato, therefore, Ficino had fulfilled the task set by Cosimo. But Cosimo was not the kind of man to let death get in the way of his work to bring the Platonic teaching into the Christian world. Ficino continues in his preface:

At the time I had done Plato into Latin, that heroic Cosimo in some way incited the heroic mind of Giovanni Pico della Mirandola, so that as it were, unwittingly, he should come to Florence. He had indeed been born in the year I undertook the translation of Plato. And then, on the same day – almost the same hour that I completed Plato – Pico came to Florence, and, immediately after our first greetings, he asked me about Plato. I will say that on this day our Plato left our house for him (*Plato huic equidem hodi liminibus nostris est egressus*). After this, vehemently congratulating me in words neither of us now remembers, he not so much persuaded as incited me to translate Plotinus. It would seem to be divinely brought about, that whilst Plato was, so to speak, being re-born, Pico was born under Saturn in Aquarius. In fact I too was born thirty years earlier under the same sign. And so, arriving in Florence on the day our Plato was produced, that old wish of the hero Cosimo, which had previously been hidden from me, was divinely inspired in Pico, and through Pico in me.

Although by nature Pico was restless and itinerant, he more or less settled in Florence, where he studied Greek with Poliziano and Platonic philosophy with Ficino. He had studied at Paris, Bologna, Ferrara and Padua, and exhausted these famous universities in his quest for all knowledge. It seems there was nothing he did not investigate: Christian theology, Neoplatonism, Zoroastrianism, Judaism. He was open-minded and in his quest befriended non-Christians such as Jews and Indian Brahmins. This quest is thought by many to have been for the perennial philosophy – that truth held in common by all faiths – but it is clear from his own writings that Pico della Mirandola was unequivocally a Christian, and what he sought was proof of the Christian religion and the divinity of Christ. The driving motivation of his life was the desire for his soul to be united with God.

Having been university trained, Pico was an adept in the schools of disputation, a combative process of logic so demanding that many men avoided university altogether. Humanism, the educational programme based on study of ancient literature, grew up outside the universities, and the Florentine Studio should perhaps be viewed more as a humanist college than a university. Of the men in our story, only Ficino and Pico had had a strict university training; Poliziano and Lorenzo were Studio trained.

Over the next two years, Pico worked on a staggering project, which was to present nine hundred theses for public disputation in Rome. This is often regarded as being an extreme act of *braggadocio*. In fact, if anything was extreme it was Pico's humility. For, having gathered up all these opinions, he now wanted to present them publicly to see which of them would survive debate. In other words, he was willing to surrender his ideas in order to find out which of them were true. Controversially, many of the theses drew on sources foreign to the Christian theologian, sources such as Hebrew, Chaldean, the *Cabbala* and natural magic. Before calling scholars to meet him, he presented his theses to the Roman Curia for approval.

During preparation for the great debate, Pico found time to write a commentary on a poem that, written by Girolamo Benivieni, set into verses Ficino's ideas on love from his book *De Amore*. Pico disagreed with Ficino on several points and planned to write his own commentary on Plato's *Symposium* sometime in the future, when he was less occupied. Meanwhile, he took the opportunity of this commentary to present his own philosophy of love, which though it closely parallels Ficino's, does not agree in all respects. He sent the work to Ficino for comment, and when it came back it had marginal comments such as 'This is a terrible mistake.' He absorbed some points of Ficino's correction but continued to argue on others and was obviously upset.

In his writings, Pico tells us that he was 'pledged to the doctrines of no man.' By this he meant that he was neither a Thomist nor a Scotist; by extension we may assume he was also neither an Aristotelian nor a Platonist. He was his own man, and he investigated all teachings to find the truth, taking from them what he found useful to support his own system of philosophy. This independence began early and was exercised on Ficino. He did not shrink from telling the renowned Platonist that he was obscure in his language and faulty in his reasoning. He also accused him of not having sufficient understanding of 'Poetic Theology' – the system employed, it is said, by the great poets such as Homer, Virgil and Dante, to veil the truth with mythic imagery. Although we can only infer this story from the guarded remarks in the writings of the two protagonists, later suppressed by their friends, one gets the impression of Ficino being somewhat less affable than usual as he slaps down this audacious young puppy.

Despite this private wrangling between teacher and pupil, and despite Ficino's expurgation of the text after Pico's death, in which all the irritated comments were removed, the *Commentary on the Canzone of Benivieni* remains a work of truth. Outlining the six steps for the liberation of the soul, it is written with stunning clarity – definition piling on definition until the soul of reader cannot help but move in response to the words. These steps, known to the Indians in the *Yoga-sutras* of Patanjali, to the Jews as *Merkabah* or Throne mysticism, and to the Sufis, are in the west an essential part of what is known as the 'gnostic' tradition deriving from Orpheus, Pythagoras and Plato, and transmitted into Christianity by Clement of Alexandria. Stage by stage they delineate the movement of the soul from the world of the senses into the pure realm of the intellect, up to the threshold of God, and, as it were, a seventh stage 'which we call the Sabbath' and about which Pico is, in this work, quiet; but which in *Heptaplus* he tells us is where God comes to the soul.

Another point of contention between Pico and Ficino was whether this final unity with God meant the death of the body. Ficino said no, Pico said yes, but he did not mean that one must die to find God, only that death will be the result of the union, for after that there would be little joy in this earthly life. The 'Mystic Death' is an element in the thought of Lorenzo and his circle which centres on the myth of Orpheus and the secrets of 'Poetic Theology', but where for the Platonists it was not literal, for Pico it was.

This then was the motivating desire of the young man making his way to Rome to prove the Christian faith in nine hundred theses, but the debate never happened. The Roman Curia declared that thirteen of the theses were erroneous; of these, three were considered heretical. Out of nine hundred this was not many, but it was enough.

In the context of the theology of the time, even the so-called heretical theses were not particularly exceptional. It may be that the Church objected to the whole project, and chose these as an excuse for cancelling it, for it enshrined a system of philosophy which seems to have been a system for self-realisation. Such a system would, of course, put man in charge of his own salvation, and rob the Church of its function. Perhaps for this reason he was condemned. Charged with heresy and faced with the imminent prospect of the Inquisition, Pico fled Italy. He was arrested in France, but following enormous diplomatic struggles between Florence and Rome, he was eventually released to live safely in Florence, at the invitation of Lorenzo and the instigation and behest of Marsilio Ficino.

Was Ficino simply forgiving, or have we in this story omitted to mention the obvious? For the facts do not make sense unless we allow for the philosophical arguments to have occurred in the context of the mutual love and respect these two men held for each other. Indeed, they seem as father and son fighting the battle fought by all fathers and sons, which is not to suggest that all fathers and sons do not love each other. When in that same 'year of the test' Pico, who so powerfully advocated chastity on the spiritual path, became a victim of the lower Venus, and, quite against his character, abducted another man's wife, it was Ficino who wrote his apology.

Angelo Poliziano

Gazing in awe on all these wild adventures was Pico's best friend, a thirty year old poet who had an aversion to scholastic philosophy. Angelo Poliziano had come to Florence as a pauper and an orphan. His brilliance in literature and languages attracted the attention of men of high standing in the city (including Benivieni and Ficino), and eventually brought him into the household of Lorenzo de' Medici. Certainly Ficino was one of his tutors at the Studio where he studied Greek and Latin. A pen-portrait that Poliziano made while a student reminds us of the breadth of knowledge required by a 'natural philosopher'. Poliziano writes to his friend, Bartolomeo Fonzio,

> Sometimes... I like to banter in composing epigrams, sometimes to couch my verses to the sweetness of a song. Quite frequently I render homage to the eloquence of the great Cicero. Then again come to me naturally the turns of prose. Sometimes, it is the appeal of a letter that arrests me, sometimes the speech composed with abundance of a great number of parts. Sometimes I become absorbed by the moral sentences written with a serene pen and by the pious words recorded in works of peace. But when I am tired of feeling pale in the shadow of the Muses, I leave the walls of my room, and go straight to the door of Matteo Franco, who is ever joking amiably, who revives in my heart a faltering strength and delivers my spirit of its black worries. Upon leaving I am met by the great Marsilio who shows no less interest in me. He unveils what immense course the wandering stars follow, why the Milky Way is so visible in a brilliant circle,

how Venus and her father exert such a favourable influence on poor mortals, why often the moon disappears, drawn off by the horses of the Night, why the rich inspiration of the Muse of the Old Man from Meonien (Homer) invented the golden chains which hang from the celestial vault, why often the airy winds wrestle on the sea, why the earth hardens under the effect of ice and cruel hail and why afterwards it splits under the action of the heat which caused Icarus to fall, why the rainbow is charged with water, why the spring sky rids itself of thunder or the shining star falls from a pure sky. Sometimes he teaches how to rid the human body of pale maladies with the help of medicines that I may be healthy; sometimes he upsets the impious theories of Lucretius who had lost his reason and sometimes he threatens to denounce the errors of Epicurius. He teaches how to reach in the fourth degree the throne of Jupiter and the brilliant planets of the celestial vault; he shows that bodies made of inert matter do not succeed, but soon once the Form of things has imperfectly disentangled itself from the material space they occupy, it is the soul which reveals itself first, inspired by the divine spirit, and finally the angelic spirit attains the vicinity of the sovereign Jupiter. Often his wise lyre chases out these grave thoughts and his voice follows the song springing up from under his expressive fingers. Like Orpheus, interpreter of Apollo's songs, Orpheus, who they say attracted the savage beasts of the Odrysae (Thracians), could with his song tame the Lions of Marmarica and the tigers who live on the black Amanus; he would make the inert rocks come down from the summit of the Caucasian mountains and the blocks of stone come from the chasms of Sicily where they are buried. Then when he has finished, drawn on by the Muse's furore I return to my usual residence, go back to composing verses, and, ecstatically invoking Phoebus, I touch the divine lyre with my plectrum.

In other words, Ficino was profoundly inspiring to a youth destined to become one of the great poets and scholars of Italy. Called by Ficino variously 'Hercules', 'Young Homer' and 'Chief Priest of the Muses', Poliziano was fully immersed in the literary tradition. Though as a student he had, as he ruefully admitted, sometimes slept during Ficino's more erudite commentaries on philosophy, he was fully awake to poetry. To him truth was to be found in the *logos*, in grammar; he believed in the sanctity of the Word. He applied himself rigorously to his studies ('painstaking' would be an understatement), seeking out error and falsehood, lies and deceptions in those texts of the ancients transmitted across the ages by scribes, translators and commentators of varying ability and intelligence. He was a giant in the new science of philology (literally, love of words) in the age which saw the advent of the printing press, and with it, as he said, 'the ability to duplicate error a thousandfold.' According to Garin, Poliziano is 'a great name in the history of the progress of human knowledge.' He was no mere scholar, however, but a consummate poet – one of those wonderful hybrids: a critic who is also a creative artist – 'divinely gifted' according to a contemporary.

That he had studied Plato, 'whose delicious name I savour as it rolls off my tongue', is evident from his works, and Ficino wrote to praise him when, during his travels in exile, Poliziano was recommending Platonic discipline to those he met in northern cities. His translation of the stoic Epictetus remains a standard text today, and in correspondence with Bartolomeo Scala defending stoicism, he makes familiar reference to Plato's *Alcibiades I*, explaining to the ex-Chancellor of Florence as if to a child why man is not the body, but the spirit which moves the body. Thus to Poliziano the Platonic wisdom was a useful, practical guide to a virtuous life. But when it came to the scholastic philosophy of the universities, he floundered in the swamps of its ugly, abstract language. Poliziano's famous aversion to philosophy, therefore, was not moral but aesthetic.

Two things served to change his heart: one was his appointment to the chair of Latin and Greek at the Studio, the other was his friendship with Pico della Mirandola. When he was appointed professor of Greek in the Studio – the first Italian to hold that chair – Poliziano was required to lecture on Aristotle, a philosopher whose works were encumbered by centuries of medieval interpreters 'who had befouled the clear waters of Aristotle with the mud of their pedantry'; in this position he could no longer indulge his abhorrence of scholastic philosophy, or justify his distaste on the grounds of the barbarity of its medieval Latin. For that was the language of his new colleagues, and he needed to learn it.

It has recently come to light that, before taking up his professorship in 1480, Poliziano turned to a monk of Santa Maria Novella for lessons in philosophy. Their meetings were recorded by the monk in the form of a dialogue, and reading it one can almost see the candles sputtering in the Priory of San Paolo as the embarrassed professor, half in shadow, asks humbly for instruction in a subject which he finds such a struggle. The master records that the pupil vigorously defended Plato against the Aristotelians, declaring that it seemed impossible to him the Plato should have erred, and that 'it is not permissible for us to find fault with him'.

Four years later, Pico entered his life, Pico the student of the schools, the throwback to medieval scholasticism, the uncompromising, ardent lover of philosophy and theology. The younger man became the guide of the professor, steering him through the linguistic mire with the clarity of thinking that was his genius. 'He (Giovanni Pico) is still with me, with whom he used to share his intimate personal thoughts and occasionally engage in merry banter. He chose me for his constant companion in his studies. He introduced me to philosophy, so that I began to take an interest in it, but not in the half awake state of mind I was in before, but with my eyes wide open and my mind watchfully alert, almost as though it had come to life at the call of his voice.'

Since in 1491 Poliziano was still claiming not 'to be a philosopher but a grammaticus', it is difficult to understand what he means, unless a 'grammaticus' is what today we would call a 'humanist'; if so, then by 'philosopher' he meant someone well versed in the scholastic disputations of the various schools of medieval Europe, and thus someone who spoke and wrote in that 'Parisian style' so painful to his sensitive ear. What Pico had shown him, however, was that he could find philosophy in philology, in the Word: that his bliss and his God were one and the same.

Although Poliziano the philosopher is, in the symbolic architecture of the Academy, assigned to the porch, that meeting place of stoics for whom philosophy is but a guide for leading a virtuous and just life, he could not have had a friend like Pico without feeling his soul being drawn, willy nilly, on the ascent towards God.

Plato Versus Aristotle

The abstruse discipline of philosophy that Poliziano tried to avoid was characterised by a long and often bitter dispute between those who favoured Aristotle and those who favoured Plato. Medieval theology had, since the time of St Thomas Aquinas, used the philosophy of Aristotle as the intellectual framework of Christian dogma. Now, in the fifteenth century, and through the work of Ficino, the teaching of Aristotle's master Plato was available for the first time in the western world; and where previously scholars had disputed on the relative merits of the two ancient Greeks, the mood now was to study both.

It was in this context that Pico and Poliziano intended to do for Aristotle what Ficino had done for Plato, which was to make a new translation worthy of the master, to strip him of his commentators and thus 'unveil' him. In the projected great work, they were to be joined by Ermolao Barbaro in Venice, but the premature death of all three of them in the same year stole this project from the world. Without putting too great a claim on it, it would at least be interesting to speculate what the course of modern Europe, and the relationship of science and faith might have been, had we been graced with that work. It is clear from Pico's extant writings that, though some of his ideas prefigure the advent of science, to him science, or 'natural philosophy', was an expression of God's will and power. Modern science, however, built on the foundations of the Aristotelians rather than on Aristotle himself, has stripped God from the picture.

The debate itself rested on the question: is God separate from his Creation, or present within it? That is to say, is God the transcendent 'One', or is he the immanent 'Being'? A quotation from the 1984 translation into English of the *Complete Works of Aristotle* may serve to show the difficulties of the debate. In the *Metaphysics* Aristotle declares that 'life also belongs to God; for the actuality of thought is life, and God is that actuality; and God's essential actuality is life most good and eternal. We say therefore that God is a living being, eternal, most good.'

This has been interpreted as meaning that the One and Being are the same, whereas Plato says the One is separate from Being. This is the key difference between Plato and Aristotle and the question still perplexes us today in the form of, 'Is God to be found in nature?' In 1492 Poliziano, who was due to lecture on the *Ethics* at the Studio, discussed the subject with Lorenzo de' Medici. As far as he could see, the Greek terms for immanence and transcendence are so close (*entelechia* and *endelechia* have only one consonant to differentiate them) that the whole debate probably rests on the slip of a pen! But Lorenzo was a thoroughgoing Platonist, wholly Ficinian in his thinking, and Poliziano soon found himself in difficulties as he attempted to defend Aristotle's point of view. He turned to Pico for help, and the result was a short treatise *De Ente et Uno* 'On Being and the One'. Pico addressed the tract to his friend, saying,

> You told me some days ago what Lorenzo de' Medici discussed with you concerning Being and the One. Supported by the reasons of the Platonists, he disputed against Aristotle, on whose *Ethics* you are giving a public commentary this year. Lorenzo is a man of such powerful and multiform mind that he seems to be suited to everything. What I especially admire in him is that he is always speaking or meditating on some literary matter, even though he is always very occupied with the republic. And since those who think that Aristotle disagrees with Plato disagree with me, who make a concordant philosophy of both, you asked both how Aristotle might be defended in this matter and also how he might agree with his master, Plato... What can I deny you? May I say that you are an almost inseparable companion, particularly in a literary matter? May I also be allowed, through you who vindicate a more elegant language, to use some words, which are not yet perhaps legally given to Latin? Still, the

newness of the subject makes such expression almost necessary, and therefore you should not look for the allurement of a more elegant style. As Manilius says, 'The subject itself refuses to be ornamented; it is content to be taught.'

One of Pico's strengths was his knowledge of Hebrew and the Old Testament, knowledge he considered incumbent on all Christian theologians to possess. From this knowledge he could point out that when God said to Abraham, 'I am that I am', He said, 'I, the One, am Being.' But in his attempt to show that Plato and Aristotle are in accord, Pico had to destroy the commonly-held idea that Plato's *Parmenides* (the key text in the debate) was a theology – a statement of the nature of God and the soul which, according to Ficino, had come to Plato through divine revelation. The view of all the Neoplatonists, including Ficino, was that it was the most sublime of the dialogues. But according to Pico, reason and historiography showed that the *Parmenides* was an exercise in dialectic. Ficino was angry again, more so this time, for Pico had equalised the two great philosophers, not by elevating Aristotle, but by cutting Plato off below the knees! Provoked into a response, he wrote a commentary to the *Parmenides*, and buried in it, at the end of chapter 49, the following remark:

> If only that wonderful youth (*mirandus ille*) had diligently considered the disagreements and discussions I treated above before he had the temerity to confront his teacher and to publicise an opinion so at odds with that of all the Platonists: to hold that the divine *Parmenides* is merely a work of logic and that Plato, followed by Aristotle, had identified the One and the Good with Being.

Ficino himself tells us that the *Parmenides* is almost incomprehensible. It must be the most challenging text to translate, for, just as the English have a variety of terms to mean 'rain', there are many Greek words for the concept of being, but Latin has only one term: 'ente'. Ficino said that, in order to understand the dialogue, one must be more than intelligent. 'Whoever is about to undertake the reading of this sacred text must first prepare himself with sobriety of soul and liberty of intelligence before daring to take up the mysteries of this heavenly work.'

That is to say, he who would understand Plato must practise Platonism; he who would understand philosophy must practise philosophy. If a man writes of divine frenzy, he must have experienced it; if Plato wrote the *Parmenides* under divine frenzy, then to read and understand, a man must bring himself to a similar condition.

Ficino's anger was such that, like blazing Apollo, he melted the presumptuous wings of Pico's Icarus. But once his anger had subsided, Ficino must have been grateful for the challenge, for the provocation, like grit in an oyster, produced a pearl of original thinking. Forced to defend the *Parmenides* as a dialogue of direct revelation from the Muses, Ficino created a reading of Plato distinct from both scholasticism and neoplatonism, as different 'as Brunelleschi's cupola from the Pantheon' as Michael Allen has observed. Nevertheless, it could be suggested (with some temerity) that, had Ficino taken note of Pico's charges of obscurity and lack of definition, his metaphysical commentaries would be less difficult for us to read today. If it were not for his wonderful letters, written in truth and simplicity, Ficino might have remained a closed book to the modern world.

But this was another argument we should not view out of context. Like Plato and Aristotle, Ficino and Pico held more in common than in difference, and rather than judge one against the other, it is best to see them, together with Poliziano, as a trinity in the evolution of human thought, the light of God pouring through each man's individual genius to bring the modern world to birth.

While Ficino believed the *Parmenides* hid beneath esoteric veils a theology which prefigures the Christian faith of the Trinity, Pico was discovering the same truth in the Hebrew system of knowledge called the *Cabbala*. It is said that the five books of the law of Moses were written for the people, but that on Mount Sinai he also received a secret law from God, to be revealed only to a few, and then orally. This law was written down by the Jews after the Babylonian exile, and this is what is called the *Cabbala*. In the *Books of Esdras*, Pico found mention of the Trinity, the Incarnation, and many other aspects of the Christian faith. This endeared him to the *Cabbala* forever. Using its techniques of interpretation on *Genesis*, he wrote a work called *Heptaplus*, dedicated to Lorenzo de' Medici, 'whose interest in the secret wisdom of Moses is well known.'

Being the first Christian to study this ancient esoteric system of the Jews, Pico is the father of Christian Cabbalism and a major figure in what is known as 'The Western Esoteric Tradition'. Cabbalism, through a system of finding numerical alternatives to Hebrew letters, provides a key to understanding the symbolism of the *Bible*. Deeper than this, however, it is a system of self-knowledge. If Pico had, as he claimed, succeeded in reconciling the philosophies of Plato and Aristotle, did he find his key to this squaring of the circle in the *Cabbala*? It seems possible; indeed, in the current edition of the *Encyclopaedia Britannica*, in the article on Jewish Mysticism, we find the following corroboration (albeit written in that language of abstraction that used to torment poor Poliziano):

At the base of the Kabbalistic view of the world there is an option of faith: it is by a voluntary decision that the unknowable deity—who is 'nothing' or 'nothingness' (nonfinite) because he is a fullness of being totally inaccessible to any human cogitation—set into motion the process that leads to the visible world. This concept radically separates Kabbala from the determinism from which the philosophy of the period could not, without internal contradictions, free the principle of being. In addition it offers a solution consistent with faith to the problem, highly embarrassing for the philosophers, of creation *ex nihilo* (out of nothing): the paradoxical reinterpretation of the concept of the 'nothing' eliminates the original matter coeternal with God and solves the opposition between divine transcendence (remoteness from the world) and immanence (presence in the world); issuing from the unfathomable depth of the deity and called to return to it, the world, visible as well as invisible, is radically separated from God, who is at the same time constantly present.

It is the duty of historians to present the facts, making them as coherent as possible; but sometimes the facts leave out something that can then only be supplied by an act of the imagination. Pico della Mirandola, who as a youth inspired Ficino to translate Plotinus, grew up to challenge some of his teacher's ideas. The same Pico persuaded Lorenzo to invite Girolamo Savonarola to Florence, and it was Savonarola who was to bring an end to Medici power, the very power that brought us Plato. Yet, despite these things, Pico never lost the affections of his friends. It is strange bordering on inexplicable that Lorenzo, having heard himself publicly denounced as a tyrant by Savonarola, retained an undimmed fondness for Pico to the very end. Even on his deathbed Lorenzo was asking for the young man to visit him, 'if he has the time'.

If this affection for Pico is difficult to understand from the facts, it is because the facts on their own are like ingredients without a binding agent. Apparent contradictions abound in the story of this group. Lorenzo, suspecting Ficino of complicity in the Pazzi Conspiracy, put him before a security committee. On the eve of Lorenzo's departure for Naples, Lorenzo had a row with Poliziano that sent the latter into voluntary exile, searching for a new patron. Ermolao Barbaro disagreed with Pico on the matter of style versus content and had to suffer an onslaught of rhetorical brilliance that must have been humiliating. But such details of conflict are matched by ones of love: when Pico abducts another man's wife, it is Ficino who lends his support; when Pico is under threat of the Inquisition, Lorenzo harbours him; as soon as Lorenzo invites him to return, Poliziano rushes back from exile to serve his patron ever after with exemplary loyalty. When they hear that Barbaro is dying of poison, Poliziano and Pico hurriedly send an expensive antidote to him in Rome, although unfortunately it arrived too late.

The binding agent is friendship, that which, according to Pico, 'the Pythagoreans say is the end of all philosophy'. The over-riding, contradictory message one receives from the correspondence between these contending intellects is that of love itself, and in very large measure. That is the context of these disputes, and the fact which the historians tend to ignore, even though Ficino himself provides the documentary evidence.

Only two years after the premature death of Lorenzo, and within two months of each other, Pico and Poliziano died. Pico was 32, Poliziano 40. In their last years, they lived as neighbours, Pico's villa a little higher up the hill of Fiesole than Poliziano's. The last letter of Poliziano was addressed to Ficino. It is the letter of a man who, along with his friend, was leaving the active life to begin a life of contemplation, although they were not so strict and monastic as to deny themselves good wine! With its sense of rest, repose and completion it is a perfect last letter, made all the more poignant by the fact that its author did not know it was his last:

> I hope when your Careggi becomes too hot in August you will not spurn this little Fiesolan country place of ours. Here we have many springs, and since we are in a narrow valley, there is little sun; certainly we are never without a breeze. The little villa lies hidden away from the road and almost in the middle of a wood, yet even so it has a view over all Florence, and although there are a great many people hereabouts, yet there is always that solitude which the contemplative love. You will also be able to have a twofold pleasure here, for often stealing unannounced from his oak grove comes Pico and, having dragged me away from my hiding place, takes me with him to dinner, which I have indeed known to be frugal but always both sensible and full of delightful conversation and amusement. Nevertheless you had better stay with me because you will not eat worse here and perhaps you will drink better, since in the matter of wines I would be a strong rival even of Pico. Vale.
> *Angelo Poliziano. August 1494, Fiesole.*

These friends of Ficino were not comfortable ones, agreeing with everything he had to say. The documentary evidence of why they were friends in the first place, and how they remained so, is to be found in Ficino's letter to Ermolao Barbaro (3/31).

'Are those who hold the same opinions necessarily friends? Not at all. For we may hold the same opinion on a great many things concerning both men and nature, and yet hate one another.' So, is the common element a shared desire? No, the sharing of goods breeds jealousy. 'But if men may be found who seek the same good, because it is infinite, because it cannot anywhere be prevented from abounding without limit, then such men would not be agitated by any enmity among themselves.' But even this, according to Ficino, is still not the ultimate secret of friendship, for men may desire the good and still not love one another. 'Where then shall we find goodwill itself, which is nothing other than to will the good, unless we find it within the compass of that good itself which is all good, that is God?' The answer follows: 'Most akin to the divine mind are minds which are dedicated to God before all else. And so, such minds are straightway drawn by ardour and sweetness of love beyond telling, towards both God and each other, as they first freely give themselves back to Him, as to a father, and then give themselves up in utter joy to each other, as to brothers. All other so-called friendships between men are nothing but acts of plunder.'

And if we still have doubts as regard to Ficino's true feeling for Pico, he wrote after the death of his young friend: ' … in age he was like a son to me, in familiarity like a brother, and in affection like a second self.'

What united these fellow philosophers was not their love of each other, or even of Plato, but their love of God. What they knew in practice and exemplified in their lives was, as Ficino said at the head of his letter to Barbaro, that 'friendship between men cannot be kindled unless God breathes upon it.'

NOTES

Sources:

> Michael Allen, *Plato's Third Eye. Studies in Marsilio Ficino's Metaphysics and its Sources.* (1995)
> Michael Allen, *Icastes: Marsilio Ficino's Interpretation of Plato's Sophist* (Oxford, 1989)
> Quirinius Breen, 'Giovanni Pico della Mirandola on the Conflict of Philosophy and Rhetoric' *Journal of the History of Ideas, Vol. XIII,* 1952

Brian P. Copenhaver and Charles B. Schmitt, *Renaissance Philosophy* (Oxford, 1992)

William G. Craven, *Giovanni Pico della Mirandola, Symbol of his Age, Modern Interpretations of a Renaissance Philosopher* (Geneva, 1981)

Eugenio Garin, *Portraits of the Quattrocento* (New York, 1972)

Jonathan Hunt, *Politian and Scholastic Logic* (a dialogue written by a Franciscan friar of Santa Maria Novella).

Original texts:

Marsilio Ficino, Preface to Latin translation of Plotinus, *Opera Omnia,* (repr. Turin, 1959)

Marsilio Ficino, *The Letters of Marsilio Ficino:* Translated from the Latin by Members of the Language Department of the School of Economic Science (London, 1975-)

Clarice de' Medici, unedited letters to Niccolo Michelozzi, collected by Natalie Tomms, a student of Prof. F.W. Kent at the University of Monash.

Giovanni Pico della Mirandola, 'Oration on the Dignity of Man,' English translation by Elizabeth Livermore Forbes, in *The Renaissance Philosophy of Man*, ed. Cassirer, Kristeller and Randall, (1975)

Giovanni Pico della Mirandola, *On the Dignity of Man, On Being and the One,* translated by C.G. Wallis, P.J.W. Miller and D. Carmichael (1965) (this translation includes *Heptaplus*)

Giovanni Pico della Mirandola, *Commentary on a Canzone of Benivieni*, translated by Sears Jayne (1984)

Giovanni Pico della Mirandola, *Conclusiones nonagentae, Le novecento Tesi dell'anno 1486*, a cura di Albano Biondi (1995).

Angelo Poliziano, *Opera Omnia* (repr. Basle, 1971)

Angelo Poliziano, 'Letter to Bartolommeo Scala in defence of Epictetus', English translation in *Cambridge Translations of Renaissance Philosophical Texts, Vol. 1: Moral Philosophy,* ed.Jill Kraye

Ficino's Influence in Europe

VALERY REES

Philosophy, to express it in a few words,
is the ascent of the mind from the lower regions
to the highest, and from darkness to light. *

TRACING the influence of a great teacher is no easy task. A single idea or image may be followed as a thread through texts and sources; memorable lines of a poet may echo through later prose and verse. But Ficino's influence is harder to trace, for two reasons. Firstly, he was not the only translator of Plato in late 15th century Florence. Important groundwork had already been done by Coluccio Salutati, Leonardo Bruni and others. The revival of the wisdom of antiquity was already being taken up enthusiastically in every shape and form. Secondly, the rôle of a teacher is to foster and encourage the talents of his pupils to prepare for new challenges they will face and solve in their own way. How this may be measured is clearly a complex matter.

Faced with this two-fold difficulty, some have undervalued Ficino's role as an educator of minds and a publicist of Platonic thought. Pasquale Villari, writing in 1888[1], paid lip service to Ficino's importance, describing how Florence 'became the resort of scholars from all parts of Italy and the studious youth of Germany, France and Spain came there on purpose to attend the lectures of Ficino; for his works were eagerly read throughout Europe ...'

But his strong bias against Ficino soon breaks through and he says of Ficino's works that 'their merits and defects, truths and errors, alike contributed to swell his popularity.'

* Ficino, *Letters*, Vol 3, letter 18

64

Unable to follow Ficino's reasoning or his conclusions, Villari displayed considerable animosity towards the man:

> Ficino was so completely absorbed by his feverish passion for study, that he became a species of living dictionary of ancient philosophy... Nevertheless these studies failed to give him habits of judgement and independent observation. Neither his own reason, the whole of nature, nor the consciousness of humanity, sufficed to guide him to the discovery of truth.

Villari was blinded to Ficino's virtues by his own idolisation of Savonarola, and for him Ficino committed the ultimate sin of parting company with Savonarola as the latter's policies became more extreme.[2] Of Ficino's *Platonic Theology*, which he describes as his 'principal work', he says,

> He sought to marshal all his doctrines in a certain logical and systematic form. But no one must expect to find in it any genuine philosophical unity. None existed in the author's mind, and all his writings take the shape of lengthy dissertations, here and there interrupted and confused by a crowd of secondary ideas gleaned from a host of different writers. Neither scientific unity nor logical sequence of thought is to be found in his works. We do not even find the elegance of style that might well be expected from an author who spent his whole life in the study of Greek literature.[3]

I am glad to say that Ficino studies over the last 50 years have entirely reversed this view in every respect. Ficino is *par excellence* the philosopher of unity, and his style shines forth as a beacon of clarity and power.

Nonetheless, I have quoted Villari at length by way of a warning, so that we do not fall into the equal and opposite error of attributing too much to one man at a time of manifest widespread achievement. Ficino himself spoke of living in golden times,[4] and he moved among poets, scholars and artists whose brilliance posterity has endorsed: Angelo Poliziano, Cristoforo Landino, Giovanni Pico della Mirandola, Lorenzo de' Medici, Alessandro Botticelli, to name but a few.

So how are we to reach a balanced view of Ficino's contribution to European thought? Each of the other essays in this book tells part of the story. What I would like to do here is to highlight a few of his most important followers outside Italy.

After Italy, the first country to receive the Renaissance was Hungary. This fact may surprise us now, for subsequent historical events weakened the bonds that were forged between Hungary and Italy at this time. But the kingdom of Hungary was far larger then than now, and played a crucial role in the defence of Europe against the Turks, who were enjoying a phase of aggressive expansion at this period. The Hungarian King, Matthias Corvinus, was an enthusiastic follower of Ficino's ideas. Conscious of his position as defender of Christendom, Matthias particularly responded to the idea of a philosopher-king as described by Ficino in expounding Plato's *Republic*. Ficino declared that only the ruler who could unite wisdom and strength in his own person could bring about a solution to the very real dangers facing Italy and Europe. He likened Matthias to a messiah.[5] Indeed, thinking rather of the role of Emperor, he suggested more than once that a union of temporal and spiritual power was necessary and that a strong king should arise to guard the whole of the Christian world.[6]

Matthias seems to have shared these views. He aspired to election as Holy Roman Emperor, though this aspiration was never realised, for he died in mid-career at the age of only 47.[7] But he embodied within himself the ideals of strong leadership, military skill, justice and learning. He was well used to the role of representing a unifying figurehead for the interests of many different national groups within his own diverse realm. Furthermore, he took seriously the responsibilities of an enlightened prince. He thirsted after knowledge and wisdom himself and he took steps to encourage the same in others. His most famous foundation was the Corvina Library, a magnificent collection of all the known works of Greek and Latin learning, a treasure house second to none outside Italy. Less widely known are his efforts to create a highly educated administrative class in both church and state, selected for ability rather than by birth alone, and his attempts to attract leading teachers to Hungary.

The two were in fact connected, for Matthias fully recognized the power of eloquence and rational thinking in promoting effective rule at every level. He himself had benefitted from reading the classics and putting into practice what he read. He was therefore very ready to promote education based on classical models. The famous German mathematician and astronomer, Regiomontanus (Johannes Müller of Königsberg) came to teach at the new university of Pozsony in 1467. Giovanni Gatti (Cardinal Bessarion's secretary) and the Polish Martin Bylica of Ilkusz, came to join him there. Between 1469 and 1471 negotiations were in hand to invite John Argyropoulos, the famous Greek scholar whom Lorenzo had managed to attract to Florence. In the event, after his release from Florence had been negotiated, Argyropoulos preferred instead to take up a lucrative post in Rome.

There were plans to expand the new university of Pozsony into a leading centre of excellence to which the finest scholars would naturally want to come. How much these plans owed to the King and how much his old tutor and Chancellor, Johannes Vitéz, is not entirely clear. Vitéz had sponsored the education in Italy of several leading courtiers, as well as overseeing that of Matthias himself as a child. But in 1472 Vitéz fell from power through his part in a conspiracy, and the university of Pozsony soon ceased to exist. Yet from the later plans for another new university in Buda, we can see the king's personal interest in education.

Interestingly, what had provoked the conspiracy of 1472 and Vitéz's fall was the king's attempt to appropriate that very kind of unified power that Ficino recommends.[8] In order to mount an effective defence against the Turks, Matthias needed a strong, disciplined and mobile army, backed by generous financial provision. He also needed security on his other borders, which could not at that time be counted on. Thus he was drawn into wars against Bohemia and the Imperial Crown, and found himself obliged to levy taxation upon Church lands and wealth for a war that had now changed from an anti-Turkish crusade to an attack on other Christian powers.

The fall of Vitéz and some other leading humanist courtiers led to a temporary mistrust on the King's part of Italian influences. But by 1476 he had relented, and his marriage to Beatrix, daughter of the

King of Naples, marked the beginning of a new phase, a re-intensification of Italian influences. In particular, a member of Ficino's intimate circle arrived in Buda as part of the Queen's retinue: Francesco Bandini. Through him a personal link was forged between the Hungarian court on the one hand and Ficino and the Academy in Florence on the other. Important books started to arrive in Hungary and to be discussed. First was Ficino's *De Christiana Religione* in 1476; then the *Life of Plato* in 1477 and two volumes of *Letters* sometime in the early 1480s. In 1479 it was Ficino's turn to be invited, like Argyropoulos, to teach in Hungary, and he was pressed again to accept in 1482. Several letters discuss this invitation, which Ficino also never took up, but his works continued to be enthusiastically received.

The *Platonic Theology* arrived in 1482, straight after publication in Florence. Ficino's translations of the *Dialogues* of Plato were sent in 1484-5, together with his Synesius *On Dreams*. In 1488 or 1489 a splendid presentation volume of Ficino's *Letters*, Books I-VIII arrived. Iamblichus' *Mysteries of the Egyptians and Assyrians* were sent as soon as the translation was ready in 1489, and finally, 1490 saw the arrival of the eagerly awaited full Plotinus translations and commentaries, Pythagoras' *Symbola* and *Golden Verses*, Porphyry's *On abstaining from animal food*, Psellus on *Daemons*, and Priscianus Lydus' *Theophrastus on the Mind*.

Most significant of all, though, was the *De Vita*, published at the end of 1489. Although dedicated to Lorenzo de'Medici as a composite work, the third and most controversial of its three books was composed especially for Matthias. This third book, entitled *On obtaining Life from the Heavens*, deals with the correspondences between the heavenly powers and human affairs, and how to harness the one in service of the other. Intrigued by a puzzling passage in Plotinus about drawing down power from the stars to infuse life into statues and figures, Ficino explores the universal forces of the heavenly world, and how these may be focused in human endeavours. Many interpretations were later laid on this book as a repository of alchemy and magic. But it is well to heed Ficino's own warning: speaking of those who have made complex diagrams or models of the movements of the heavenly bodies, he says,

But I leave this to those who make images. You, however, will fashion a better image within yourself when you know that nothing is more orderly than the heavens and that nothing can be thought of that is more temperate than Jupiter; you should hope at last to attain benefits from the heavens and from Jupiter if you have rendered yourself very orderly and temperate in your thoughts, emotions and mode of life.[9]

Also popular in Buda were two other works. One of these arrived in 1469, long before the rest, because it was sent not to the King but to Janus Pannonius, nephew of Vitéz and Bishop of Pécs, who had visited Ficino in Florence. It was an early dedication copy of Ficino's commentary on Plato's *Symposium*, the *De amore* or *Commentary on Love*. Its recipient, Janus, had spent some time in Florence, and had been as impressed by a codex of Plotinus in Vespasiano's bookshop, as by meeting Ficino. The other work, whose arrival in Hungary cannot be dated, was Ficino's translation of Hermes Trismegistus. A Greek text of this work had pride of place in the Greek section of the Corvina Library. It is a work that speaks of man's divine nature in powerful poetic imagery, and of how, through the intelligence of the heart, the human soul may be reunited with the source of all.

Several leading Hungarians came within Ficino's circle of friends and acquaintances.[10] Other influential figures at the Hungarian court were deeply imbued with Ficino's ideas.[11] Italian poets of Ficino's circle also came to look after the Corvina Library, and to tutor his son, Janus Corvinus.[12] Many other Florentines also visited Hungary on official business or in hope of new opportunities.

In the short term, Ficino's influence provided a philosophical underpinning for the Renaissance concepts of kingship and courtly life that established themselves in Hungary. These were also expressed in an exuberant flowering of architecture, music and literature. From the Hungarian court these spread to Poland and Bohemia, and took root there. But for the long term effects of Ficino's influence on Hungarian society, we have to pick over the ruins of a society wrecked by subsequent war and destruction, for within forty years most of Hungary had fallen to the Turks, and the crown to the Habsburgs.[13] Yet Ficino's concerns were with the soul, with philosophy, love, contemplation, worship and contact with the divine. His chief influence was perhaps upon the spiritual consciousness of a generation. The two principal areas in which we may find its visible trace are in the thriving educational system that emerged phoenix-like during the period of Turkish suzerainty in Transylvania, and in the legend that took root after his death of 'Matthias the Just'.[14] This was the memory of Matthias the Philosopher-King, who had set a standard of resourcefulness, rationality and personal bravery that became deeply enmeshed both in the folklore and in the codes of honour of governing Hungarian society. As Ficino said,

> true philosophers, having recovered their wings through wisdom and justice, as soon as they have left the body, fly back to the heavenly kingdom. In heaven they perform the same duties as on earth. United with God in truth, they rejoice. United with each other in freedom they give thanks. They watch over men dutifully, and as interpreters of God and as prophets, what they have set in motion here they complete there. They turn the minds of men towards God. They interpret the secret mysteries of God to human minds.[15]

The purpose of reviving the philosophic disciplines of the Greeks was the reinvigoration of religion. In 1483 Ficino wrote, 'We are led to truth by a two-fold path, that of authority and reason.'[16] The authority is Christ, but for reason one must turn to Platonic philosophy, which of course by 1490 embraced Chaldaean and Egyptian and several Greek sources, all now accessible in Latin translation. It was this blend that was to prove so potent an influence elsewhere too.

In France Ficino corresponded with two members of the de Ganay family, one of whom was the president of the French Parlement.[17] Lefèvre d'Etaples, priest and professor of philosophy in Paris from 1490, took up Ficino's teachings with great enthusiasm. He added commentaries to Ficino's Hermes translation as early as 1494, and a second edition appeared in 1505 including a preface by Briçonnet. Lefèvre went on to produce important religious and philosophical works of his own, and was drawn towards the development of a potent blend of mysticism and reform thinking that was to exert considerable influence on Luther. Lefèvre's influence in France was significant, especially on younger scholars. Briçonnet meanwhile rose to a leading position in the church, becoming Bishop of Meaux from 1516. The group of reformers that gathered round him combined Platonic ideas with a renewed study of the *Bible*, especially the *Epistles* of St Paul that had been so dear to Ficino's heart and on which he was still writing commentaries when he died in 1499. Briçonnet also became 'spiritual father' to Marguerite of Navarre, sister of King Francis I, an important patron of humanism and reform as well as being herself a writer of considerable influence. In a parallel development, also fed by Lefèvre's translations and Ficino's work, Charles de Bovelles pursued the development of religious and scientific thought in combination, seeing mathematical propositions as part of an ascent to the divine:

> One truth shines out in all things ... towards which one ascends by means of certain steps... It is the true service of God. I ask you, what more direct, more abstract or purer analogies can be furnished than mathematical writings, which show no trace of anything base, or of the flesh?[18]

French interest in Ficino was further nourished by a French translation of his *Commentary on Love* by Simon de la Haie in 1545, followed in 1578 by *The Christian Religion* and a new version of the *Commentary on Love* by Guy Lefèvre de la Boderie.

By 1578, Ficino's ideas had gained adherents all over Europe by more indirect transmission through the prose of Baldassare Castiglione's *Courtier* (written in 1513-18, published in 1528), the verse of Pietro Bembo (especially *Gli Asolani*, 1505) and the dialogues of Leone Ebreo (*Dialoghi d'Amore*, written 1501-2, first published in 1535, but re-published many times thereafter). Renaissance concepts of love and courtly life had blossomed throughout the courts of Europe.

In England, Thomas Elyot's translation of the *Courtier* into English

Friend to Mankind

in 1531 had had immense success. Ficino's ideas as taken up by Spenser and ultimately Shakespeare have been discussed elsewhere in this volume. But reference to the English after-life of Ficino's philosophy would not be complete without mention of the Cambridge Platonists. In the mid-17th century, new efforts to reconcile religion and reason arose in response to the development of science. In truth, Ficino's influence can be seen on both sides of that apparent confrontation, for underlying the scientific developments of the early 17th century one may also detect both Hermeticism and Socratic enquiry. But it was to his religious thinking that the Cambridge Platonists looked to work out a new balance between the demands of the mind and the needs of the soul, avoiding both a mechanistic view of the universe and the harsh political theories of Hobbes. Benjamin Whichcote, Ralph Cudworth and Henry More are the best known of this group. They emphasised man's rational nature and the good, viewing man as capable of participation in divine wisdom. The metaphysical poets George Herbert, Henry Vaughan and Thomas Traherne inherited Ficino's philosophy of love and the soul. Ficino's legacy can also be seen in the formation of the Royal Society in 1660, with its far-reaching influence on the development of the English language and of scientific thinking. Isaac Newton, elected to membership of the society in 1671, owed much to his readings of that very Hermetic tradition which Ficino had brought back to life two hundred years before.

Either through his correspondence with Paul of Middelburg, or by some other means, Ficino's reputation reached the Netherlands,[19] and his work found many echoes in developments there. The Brethren of the Common Life, a movement which had its roots in the tradition of St Augustine, shared his contemplative approach and nurtured Erasmus (1466-1536). At Deventer, Greek was taught from the 1490s. Rudolph Agricola of Frisia (1443-85) formed a flourishing humanist academy and taught at Heidelberg. Juan Luis Vives (1492-1540), whose educational ideas were adopted in England, was originally a Spaniard, but lived mainly in Bruges.

In the German principalities, Ficino had connections with Eberard, Duke of Wurttemburg and with George Herivart, a German

Augustinian. With Martin Prenninger, professor of law at Tübingen university, Ficino conducted a rich exchange of letters that fills large sections of the later books of correspondence. Ficino's writings on astronomy and magic were also particularly admired in the intellectual circles of Germany. Jakob Böhme (1575-1624) was inspired to unite alchemical mysticism with strongly biblical religious thinking. Ficino's influence in its Hermetic guise spread rapidly through the burgeoning pre-scientific societies including the Rosicrucians (17th century). But another path of influence was through two visitors to Ficino's Academy in Florence: Johannes Reuchlin, the Reformer (1455-1522), who pioneered Hebrew scholarship and had a powerful influence on reformation thought (though repudiating its eventual break with the Catholic church), and Conrad Celtis the poet (1459-1508), founder of the several literary academies, the *Sodalitates Danubiana, Rhenana* and *Vistulana*.

Of other European lands – Spain, Portugal, Norway, Sweden and Denmark– there is less to say, though perhaps the tale is simply not yet told. Meanwhile in Italy itself, Ficino's influence took root everywhere. By far the greatest number of his correspondents were fellow Italians. His writings were particularly well received in Venice, where Aldus Manutius printed editions of Ficino's works and founded his own academy, and in the small duchy of Urbino, immortalised in Castiglione's *Courtier*, whose influence on European culture was far greater than its small size would suggest. After the French invasion of Italy in 1494, troubled times caused many setbacks to the patronage of academic life, though Renaissance arts continued to flower especially in Rome. But it was in new homes beyond the Alps that Ficino's Florentine legacy bore its richest fruits as the years advanced, and his commentaries and translations adorned the shelves of libraries all over Europe. As late as the 1880s Ficino's translations were still the basis for the most 'modern' approaches to Plato. Even today, some scholars claim that his understanding of Plotinus has never been surpassed. Though we now approach these Greek writers more directly, and in our own vernaculars, we still have much to learn from Ficino's own writings, which are truly a common European inheritance.

NOTES

1. *Life and Times of Girolamo Savonarola*, by Professor Pasquale Villari, translated by Linda Villari, written in Florence but published in London and New York, 1888, dedicated to no less a personage than William Gladstone.

2. As Villari saw it, he 'praised and admired the Friar in the days of his prosperity, and then – after the fashion of the other learned men – basely forsook and betrayed him in his time of peril.' *Ibid.*, p. 68.

3. *Ibid.* pp. 60-61.

4. Ficino wrote to Paul of Middelburg, physician and astronomer, in September 1492:
'We should call our age golden, for undoubtedly it is, since it brings forth golden spirits in profusion. No one will have the least doubt of this who cares to consider the amazing discoveries of our time. For this golden age has brought back to light the liberal arts which were almost extinct: grammar, poetry, oratory, painting, sculpture, architecture, music and the ancient art of singing to the Orphic lyre; and all this in Florence. In addition this age has returned something that was honoured in ancient times but has since almost been destroyed, that is wisdom accompanied by eloquence and prudence by military skill... In you also, my dear Paul, this age seems to have perfected astronomy, and in Florence it has recalled from darkness to light the Platonic discipline. Also in our times machines to print our books have been invented. Moreover tables have been created in which in one hour the configuration of the heavens is revealed for a whole century, not to mention a Florentine machine which reproduces the daily motion of the planets...' *Opera Omnia*, Basel, p.1133.

5. In the Preface to Book III of his Letters (Vol. 2 of *The Letters of Marsilio Ficino*, London, 1978, pp.3-5.)

6. This suggestion is found in Dante's *De Monarchia* which Ficino translated from Latin into Italian and also in his own commentary on Plato's *Statesman*.

7. Some thought he was poisoned, accusing his Queen, though contemporary descriptions of his death suggest a possible stroke.

8. See note 6.

9. Marsilio Ficino, *Three Books on Life*, tr. Kaske and Clark, Binghamton, 1989, p. 347.

10. Chief among these were Nicholas Báthory, Bishop of Vác; Peter Váradi, secretary of the royal chancery and later High Chancellor

and Archbishop of Kalocsa; the poet and writer Peter Garázda and of course the King himself.

11. Francesco Bandini, and Giovanni of Aragon, son of King Ferrante of Naples and thus the Queen's brother, who was Cardinal and primate of Hungary from 1480-85.

12. Bartolomeo della Fonte was a close friend of Ficino's. Taddeo Ugoleto was in charge of the library from 1485-90 and tutor to Janus Corvinus, Matthias' illegitimate and only son. Ugolino Verino was in Hungary 1483-4. Taddeo Ugoleto also became tutor to Janus Corvinus.

13. After Matthias' death, Janus Corvinus was not able to establish his succession. Hungary was an elective monarchy, and the nobles chose to elect a weak foreign king and to undo many of Matthias' reforms. These unwise policies led ultimately to a Peasants' revolt, the dismantling of Matthias' army and a crushing defeat by the Turks in 1526. The young king Louis II and many of the nobility died on the battle field and the Habsburgs inherited the Crown. Hungary was split into three, the western part absorbed by the Habsburgs, the southern part under full Turkish occupation and Transylvania under Turkish suzerainty.

14. After his death Matthias soon took on the stature of an Arthurian figure in Hungarian folk history, and the saying arose 'Matthias is dead, justice has died.'

15. Ficino to the Count of Gazzoldo in a letter included in the pair of volumes dedicated to King Matthias, *The Letters of Marsilio Ficino*, Vol. 3, London, 1981 p. 31. The quotation at the head of this article is also from this letter.

16. Letter to Archbishop Niccolini, *The Letters of Marsilio Ficino*, Vol. 6, 21,London, 1999.

17. He also wrote a letter to the French King Charles VIII, but this is more of an oration, aimed to deflect him from invading Italy.

18. From the dedication, to Briçonnet's father, of Lefèvre's 1514 edition of the works of Nicholas of Cusa (1401-64), German theologian and papal representative, whose work Ficino knew and supported as they shared many of the same concerns.

19. Although Paul originated from Middleburg in the Province of Zeeland, he was in Italy from the mid-1470s and became philospher, physician and astrologer to the Court of Urbino from 1479 to 1494. Ecclesiastical and diplomatic exchanges between the Netherlands and Italy were frequent.

Ficino on the Nature of Love and the Beautiful

JOSEPH MILNE

For true love is nothing other than
a certain effort of flying up to divine beauty*

THROUGHOUT the history of Western philosophy there have been several seminal moments. At these moments philosophy not only takes on a new life but the whole culture also gains new vigour. Learning and the arts flourish. Life is charged with fresh significance. The human spirit shines in amazing creativity. Yet such moments are hardly predictable from the conditions that immediately precede them. They appear to occur spontaneously. Nor is it obvious that philosophy is, so to speak, the mother of such moments. And in the case of the Renaissance it has taken scholars a long time to realise that it was a philosophical renewal that produced the soil in which the astounding flowering of the arts in the 15th and 16th centuries was born. This essay will attempt to give some insight into the importance of Ficino as a philosopher and show how his understanding of love and the beautiful inspired the poets and artists of the Renaissance.

With few exceptions, contemporary philosophers look back upon the history of philosophy as a pursuit enclosed upon itself, concerned with matters that do not touch the lives of ordinary people. And those who do not engage in philosophical studies tend to regard philosophy as a kind of sterile intellectual game of arguments, abstractions and obscure logical distinctions. These two ideas reinforce each other, and

* Ficino, *Commentary on Plato's Symposium on Love*

because of them the Renaissance is often considered as philosophically without interest. This notion is further reinforced by the artificial separation made between theology and philosophy by historians of philosophy. Thus, for example, studies are made of the philosophy of theologians of the Middle Ages which leave out of account their theological foundations and context. For this kind of history of philosophy Ficino presents a very difficult case, since he tightly draws together theology and philosophy and regards the philosophical love of truth and spiritual desire for God to be one and the same thing. In doing this, Ficino calls upon the whole of Western philosophy and theology and creates a new synthesis which we call Christian Platonism. Again, the historians of philosophy discard this new synthesis on the grounds that it is merely a retelling of ancient philosophy and offers nothing new or original. So the history of philosophy tends to leap from Aquinas to Descartes as marking significant moments. Descartes is thought significant because he brings the question of philosophical method centre stage, and in many ways since Descartes philosophy has remained preoccupied with method rather than with what previous philosophy regarded as its concern, which was knowledge of truth. Thus the study of philosophy in the English-speaking universities in our times is largely concerned with the history of philosophical method. On the Continent it is not quite the same. There philosophers, such as Husserl, Jaspers, Heidegger and Ricoeur, have been working to shift the ground of philosophy back to questions of ultimate truth and distinguish its approach from that of the natural sciences.

These are the main reasons why the philosophy of Ficino has long been overlooked. Ficino simply was not concerned with the kinds of matters later philosophy regarded as significant. Ficino, like Plato and Plotinus whom he revived through his translations, and like the great Medieval theologians such as Augustine, John Scottus Eriugena, Bonaventure and Aquinas, were concerned to penetrate the deepest mysteries of life and at the same time to lift the human spirit into a state of purity and illumination that brought the soul back to God, the source of its being. And like each of his predecessors he was concerned to explain the journey of the soul in that return to its origin.

The notion that the human soul is created in order that it should find its way back to its home in the Divine presupposes, obviously, an anthropology that acknowledges an immortal and divine essence which is human nature. It also presupposes a cosmic scheme in the creation of the universe which, in some manner, discloses the Divine. Thus Ficino belongs to the 'emanationist' school of Christian theology, like Augustine and Eriugena, rather than the 'creationist' school. As a generalisation we may say that the Christian mystics, like Bonaventure and Meister Eckhart, belong to the emanationist school, while the anti-mystical Christians belong to the creationist school. The essential difference between them is that the emanationists perceive the created world as God disclosing Himself, as becoming immanent, while the creationists perceive the created world as wholly distinct from and other than God, as outside God. Thus one school understands a unity between God and creation, while the other is dualist and holds that the Being of God and the being of the world are entirely independent. These two views have always been in conflict within the Christian tradition and still are.

This anthropology and emanationist view lies at the heart of Ficino's philosophy and also at the heart of Renaissance art. Through it Ficino reconciles the hierarchical order of the cosmos belonging to Medieval Christianity with Plato's cosmology, in which the different realms of the universe are seen as disclosing the infinite in descending order through the finite. But while the Medieval hierarchy tended eventually to freeze into a series of abstract realms, remote from ordinary human experience and with God as a passive witness, Ficino perceived it as united through the creative power of Love. Ficino marries the Christian understanding of love with the Platonic. This is by no means the first great reconciliation between Christianity and Platonism - or between Revelation and philosophy. Clement of Alexandria had done so in the third century, Augustine in the fifth, Eriugena in the ninth and Bonaventure in the thirteenth. It is characteristic of the Christian religion that it continually works to understand revelation because, although it holds that Christ is the full revelation, deficient in no part, the *human* task of grasping that full revelation is ongoing and each generation must work to grasp it anew and according to its own circumstances. However, what is new with Ficino is his philosophical understanding of the nature of Love as the active creative principle which both generates all the multiplicity of nature and which draws the human soul back to God. Love is at once the power that generates and that regenerates.

But if love is to perform this double role – the role of generating the multiplicity of all things and returning the soul to its original unity in God - there must be but one true object of love in either direction, for love cannot have two objects or ends. According to Ficino this object is Absolute Beauty, which is the radiance of God. Ficino understands the Absolute Beauty that Socrates speaks of in the *Symposium* as disclosing that aspect of God which shines in all things, and which attracts all things to itself. Beauty is not an abstract thing but perceivable, by degrees, by every being. Love moves every being, and love desires final rest in Beauty. Magnificent as are the Medieval contemplations on the ineffability, transcendence, pure being and mystery of the Divine Trinity, these contemplations no longer touched the life of man in his daily tasks and aspirations. They had become hard thoughts. But love and beauty were things that every human being knew in their hearts. What Ficino does is display the sacred aspect of them, and in so doing resolves the apparent conflict between natural desires and the desire for truth and the love of God. It is a tendency in all religions to fall into notions of a conflict between human desire and the Divine will. This divides man and curbs his spirit, as it also divides God from His creation. Once again, the great Christian mystics each present ways of overcoming this division, and Ficino draws upon these in his interpretation of Plato's philosophy of love as expounded in the *Symposium*. One might say that resolving this conflict is precisely the point where philosophy works as the handmaid to Divine Revelation, as it was understood in the Middle Ages. It is the point where faith and reason, to use Aquinas's terms, fruitfully converge. And when philosophy becomes merely a seeking of proofs for the existence of God it loses its way. For Ficino, as for Plato, reason is most itself when it is fired by love – thus the word philosophy is rightly understood as the love of wisdom.

Ficino's understanding of love is consonant with Aquinas who asserts that all things naturally seek their own good. Clearly nothing seeks its own destruction. Everything strives for the fullest actualisation of itself. Everything holds to its own being and prizes being above everything. This dynamic aspect of being (since being is not a static thing) is an activity of love. In striving for its fullest actualisation everything loves itself. Why should things be at enmity with themselves? But love also goes out of itself. It has a self-transcending element. And so all things not only cleave to their own being but seek union with all things. Thus all creatures seek to generate and nurture their offspring. Thus nature seeks a harmony between all creatures. Love also seeks to bring all things into itself, and so we speak of whatever we love as living in our hearts. What we love we hold close and protect. But also all meanness and greed may be seen as a deficiency of love, of love introverted and diminished. Those who do not love are not loved. Love thrives in its own abundance. These are all Christian insights into the nature of love as it appears in nature, in the created order. It is the dynamic power of nature. For Ficino these aspects of love are instances, visible to all, of the Divine Love which emanates from God as the life and will of all things. Just as natural love goes out of itself, so it also ascends to God in seeking final rest in God's perfection. This manifests in the philosopher's love of truth. But equally it manifests in the artist's and poet's love of beauty, for the beauty that shines in nature, in craft, in language and in thought derives from the Absolute Beauty of which these are aspects or reflections. Here lies the connection between the philosophy of Ficino and the flowering of the arts in the Renaissance.

If this love of beauty is indeed the link between the natural world and the Divine, then the question arises: how is a distinction to be drawn between the generative aspect of love, which proceeds into multiplicity, and the divine aspect which leads back to Unity? The answer lies in Ficino's understanding of how beauty generates love. In his commentary on the *Symposium* he says:

This divine beauty has generated love, that is, a desire for itself, in all things. Since if God attracts the World to Himself, and the World is attracted, there exists a certain continuous attraction (beginning from God, emanating to the World, and returning at last to God) which returns again, as if in a kind of circle, to the same place whence it issued. And so one and the same circle from God to the World and from the World to God is called by three names. Inasmuch as it begins in God and attracts to Him, it is called Beauty; inasmuch as emanating to the World it captivates it, it is called Love; inasmuch as returning to its author it joins His work to Him, it is called Pleasure. Love, therefore, beginning from Beauty, ends in Pleasure. This was expressed in that famous hymn of Hierotheus and Dionysius the Areopagite, where these theologians sang as follows: 'Love is a good circle which always revolves from the Good to the Good.' For Love is necessarily good since it is born from the Good and returns to the Good.[1]

Love arises, then, from beauty holding to itself and yet going out from itself and finally returning to itself. So the generating aspect of love, though it brings forth the multiplicity of the world and all creatures, seeks its final rest in its source, beauty. Beauty holds to itself because it is the splendour of the divine goodness, and goodness cannot ever become other than itself.

There is an important philosophical principle here. In the created realms all things are in motion, or as Plato says, always becoming. But in the divine realm that which is, truly is and therefore it is at rest in complete fullness of being. It has no deficiency and so there is nothing for it to become. If it were to undergo any change, such change could only be a deficiency, becoming less in some way. It is so absolutely itself that it has no distinction in itself, no quality, no attribute, no tendency, and so is rest itself. Thus it is called the One because the One is not made up of any parts and so is indivisible. All the names given to God, as Dionysius observes in *The Divine Names*, attempt in some way to indicate this self-sufficiency and absolute rest, even though the mind cannot grasp such oneness because by nature it apprehends only distinctions and opposites. The One, or God, is not opposite to anything, nor is it a union of opposites in any way. It is that which ontologically precedes and causes all such distinctions. Truth is of the same kind, and every particular truth is true in so far as it manifests or reflects absolute Truth itself, though absolute Truth itself cannot be conceived by the mind. Yet the mind discerns particular truths because it orients itself towards absolute Truth itself. Truth is the rest that the intellect seeks, and so it is absolute Truth that attracts the intellect, from above itself, even though it cannot grasp it in any form, object or conception. So intellect is obedient to truth and serves truth, and in this way it transcends itself. Goodness is also of the same kind. Beauty, truth and goodness, the Platonic trinity, are three ways of speaking of the same thing. They are absolute by the fact that they admit of no opposites and cannot be compared with anything nor mixed with anything. Philosophically this is what makes them metaphysical principles. All distinctions and all relations belong to the created order.

Yet the One is not, so to speak, imprisoned within itself. Precisely because it is without attribute it is unlimited, and so it can go forth from itself while remaining wholly at rest within itself. Because it is One it can disclose the multiple. This is a mystery that has been expressed in many ways by the theologians. Bonaventure, for example, expresses it in terms of superabundance within the dynamic union of the Divine Trinity in which the Father completely imparts Himself to the Son and the Son empties Himself into the Holy Spirit. Thus the Son is the Word of the Father and the Holy Spirit is the reception of the Word. In this eternal disclosure of Himself within Himself to Himself is God's infinite self-knowing, and out of the abundance of this self-knowing comes forth the creation as God saying Himself in the multitude of semblances of His imageless being. Ficino expresses this theological mystery through the motion of love cleaving to the beautiful. Love is therefore understood as the seat of all desire. 'For it is the same God whose beauty all things desire, and in possessing whom all things rest. From there, therefore, our desire is kindled.'[2]

But just as all things seek their rest in God, and that is what they most desire, so they seek their own perfection. Desire, in this pure state, is in no way selfish. God does not desire that creatures should cease to be in their thirst for union with Him. If they ceased to be when they finally came to rest in God, then God would not be giving Himself to them. But Ficino understands that God has already given Himself to every creature by being their own centre. 'Who will deny that God is rightly called the center of all things since He is present in all things, completely single, simple, and motionless?'³ This self-giving of God as the centre of every being follows naturally from Ficino's understanding of creation as emanation and as an act of infinite love. If God did not give Himself to created beings, then they would be absolutely separate from and alien to God and creation would be a kind of shunning of God from Himself in that He would be making a difference from Himself. If God made a difference from Himself He would negate His own infinity. Ficino explains this imparting of God's centre as the centre of every being through the analogy of the lines radiating from the centre of the circle:

And just as the center point is found everywhere in the lines and in the whole circle, and through its own point each of the lines touches the mid-point of the circle, so God, the center of all things, who is the simplest unity and the purest act, puts Himself into all things, not only because He is present to all things, but also because to everything created by Him He gave a certain inmost potency, most simple and most distinctive, which is called the unity of that thing, from which and to which, as from and to their own center the rest of the parts and potencies of the thing hang. Clearly it is proper that created things collect themselves to this their own center, to this their own proper unity, before they cling to their creator, in order, as we have now often repeated, to be able, by clinging to their own center, to cling to the center of all things. ⁴

Desire, then, the natural offspring of love, manifests in all created beings as their power of collecting into their own centre and unity, and out of that unity rising above themselves to the centre and unity of all things. So pure desire involves no negation of anything. It is only when this pure desire becomes misdirected or limited that it appears, in a particular being striving for its own exclusive satisfaction, to conflict with the universal desire of all beings to unite together in God. Love, then, is understood as the power that draws every being into its own unity and autonomy, into becoming wholly itself, and at the same time draws it to union with God. And the attracting power of this love is Beauty understood as God's infinite goodness manifest as the splendour of all things. In this way love is seen to overcome the apparent duality of God and creation. By contemplating the nature of love and the end it ultimately seeks we discover a dynamic principle of unity at work throughout the realms of creation which overcomes the dualism that appears when regarding created things merely as static objects, since as static objects they appear discrete and separate. It is worth noting in this regard how modern attempts to discern the divine in the material world through the scientific method usually discard in advance any teleology or aim in nature, and so no unifying principle can be discerned. The question of the unity of nature is really a philosophical question, and as such it properly belongs to every human being rather than to just one discipline.

There is another principle to be discerned in this understanding of love. If every being is drawn by love to beauty, then there must be a knowledge of beauty within every being by which it knows beauty. But also, beauty will unite only with the beautiful, for 'likeness generates love.'[5] So only the beautiful will unite with the beautiful. This is also the case with the other eternal principles, such as truth or goodness. Following Plato, Ficino understands that the intellect could not seek the true if the true were not already implanted in the soul, since without an innate knowledge of it there would be no means of discerning it.

> Who will deny that the soul immediately from a tender age desires the true, the good, the virtuous, and the useful? But no one desires things which are unknown to him. Therefore there are in the soul some notions of those things even before it desires them, through which, as Forms or Reasons of the things themselves, it judges them to be desirable.[6]

In discussing how these forms and reasons are in the soul, Ficino remarks that Plato appears to suppose they are 'painted on the substance of the soul, as it were, like pictures on a wall.'[7] Augustine holds a view similar to this in his understanding of the soul being formed in the image of the Divine Trinity. But if the soul is formed in the divine image, then that image must be impressed upon the soul directly by God, otherwise the soul would seek only the images of divine things and not the divine itself. So likewise with truth or goodness. The soul would seek only likenesses of these if only likenesses were impressed upon it. It would never seek truth or goodness itself and so remain always separated from them. So Ficino refers to the *Republic* where Plato says that:

...the light of the intellect for understanding all things is the same God himself, by whom all things were made. For he compares the sun and God to each other in this way: as the sun is to our eyes, so God is to our intellects. The sun creates our eyes and gives them the power of seeing, which would be useless and sunken in eternal darkness if the light of the sun were not there, painted with the colours and shapes of objects, in which light the eye sees the colours and shapes of objects. The eye does not see anything except light. However, it seems to see various objects, because the light which pours into it is charged with various shapes of external objects. The eye certainly can look at this light reflected in objects, but it cannot bear to look at the light itself as its source.[8]

It is by this light that the forms and reasons are within the soul.

The whole fertility of the soul clearly consists in this: that in its inner being shines that eternal light of God charged with the Reasons and Ideas of all things; the soul can turn to this light whenever it wishes, through purity of life and intense concentration of desire, and when it has so turned, it shines with the sparks of the Ideas.[9]

Thus the soul is not merely impressed with images of truth at one remove from God, but is lit by the eternal light of God directly and perceives the nature of created things by this light. It follows from this that the more the intellect seeks truth and goodness the closer it conforms to its own nature and the nearer it approaches its own origin in God. This is also how the soul knows the universals, since it is the eternal light that discloses every particular form in relation to its universal Idea which resides in the light itself.

This theory of knowledge, founded in the principle of unifying love, is philosophically very significant because it overcomes the subject-object dualism prevalent in philosophy since Descartes and elaborated further by Kant. According to Ficino, the real knowledge of things lies in uniting with their centre or essence, and their centre corresponds with their centre in God. Such knowledge comes through love because it is only love that desires things for and in themselves. Philosophy falls short of real knowledge so long as it seeks only conceptions and definitions of things. Love, on the other hand, since it gives birth to all things, also gives birth to their true knowledge, which is what they are in the mind of God. This philosophy of love was given full expression by the Renaissance artists. It is the key to the poetry and songs of the Renaissance. In England it was perfected in the songs of John Dowland and the love comedies and *Sonnets* of Shakespeare. Who else than the divinity within are those Sonnets addressed to? It is strangely appropriate that this philosophy should shine through the arts since the one regret of Socrates in has last days was that he had neglected to play the lyre.

Through studying Ficino we not only discover the moving force of the arts of the Renaissance, we also find our way back to a philosophical and theological synthesis that reconnects us with the great richness of the Western philosophical tradition. We see, from the artists and thinkers who consulted Ficino, that philosophy is indeed a wellspring of inspiration, culture and creativity.

NOTES

1. Ficino, *Commentary on Plato's Symposium on Love*, translated by S. Jayne, Connecticut, 1994, p. 46.
2. *Ibid.* p. 46
3. *Ibid.* p. 48
4. *Ibid.* p. 48
5. *Ibid.* p. 56.
6. *Ibid.* p. 132
7. *Ibid.* p. 134
8. *Ibid.* p. 134
9. *Ibid.* p. 135

Ficino and Astrology

GEOFFREY PEARCE

*Applying ourselves to astrology, we carefully considered the
last conjunction of Saturn and Mars in Virgo, and the next
one. We also considered the next entrance of the Sun into
Aries and the beginnings of the quarters of the whole year.
In addition, we considered the eclipse of the Moon in
Aquarius, as well as the future eclipse of the Sun in Leo and
other eclipses for the following year. Finally, we considered
the discordant combination of Mars and Jupiter, besides much
else. We have concluded from all this that the next two years
will be so miserable it will be commonly believed that the
utter destruction of the world is imminent, a universal and
final calamity overwhelming the human race by war,
pestilence and famine.* *

It may seem strange to the modern reader for the Italian philosopher,
theologian and linguist, whose writings generated the Florentine
Renaissance that influenced European thought for centuries, to have a
knowledge of astrology. The fact that he makes known his conversance
with the subject in letters to the Pope, some of his Cardinals, King
Matthias Corvinus of Hungary, the Venetian Ambassador and other
eminent men throughout the continent, may appear to be even more
remarkable.

However, Ficino was a man of his time. By the end of the 14th century,
and for most of the 15th century, the courts of Europe, both lay and
ecclesiastical, had astrologers as important advisors. They were consulted
by everyone from the Emperor downwards. Their function was not to

---

* Ficino, *Letters*, Vol 5, letter 9, to Pope Sixtus, 25 December 1478 say what was going to happen in future, but rather when was a propitious time for starting a war, or some new venture, besides casting natal charts for the royal family and some of their retinue. It was a period when the lay nobility accepted the validity of divination techniques of all kinds, as did the uneducated masses listen to the numerous soothsayers. Certainly no-one doubted the value of astrology to medicine. It constituted a quarter of the four year medical course at the University of Bologna, one of the oldest universities in Europe.

Astrology's general acceptance came from the writings of the leading theologians and academics of the Middle Ages, such as Thomas Aquinas, Bonaventure, Scotus, and Ockham. These men accepted Aristotle's view of the universe and his ideas on what constituted *scientia*, that is, knowledge, which formed the six liberal arts taught in Schools and Universities, and the basic philosophy of educated men. Aristotle said that all sublunary change was the result of and dependent upon the motions in the heavens. This meant that astrology was accepted as a part of *astrologia* – or *Astronomia*. Astronomy and astrology were both integral parts of one science, which played a part in medicine, meteorology, alchemy, and remedies against ill-fortune, such as gemstones and amulets.

However, there was fierce opposition against astrology from some members of the clergy. The proposition that man's psychological and physical make up, as well as his actions, could be subjected to planetary influences conflicted with their beliefs in his freewill and responsibility to God. So Ficino had to be careful in his writings particularly as, in 1473, he was made a priest.

Ficino acknowledged that it would seem strange for a member of the Church to believe in astrology when he wrote around 1474 in a letter to Rinaldo Orsini, Archbishop of Florence 'People will perhaps laugh at a priest who heeds astronomy. But I, relying on the authority of the Persians, Egyptians, and Chaldeans, considered that while earthly matters were indeed the concern of others, heavenly matters in truth were the sole concern of the priest.'[1]

In his extensive correspondence covering over thirty years up to the mid-1490s, Ficino includes numerous astrological references, and appeals to the wisdom contained in the stars. His writings show considerable knowledge of the subject. This came from a potpourri of sources through his translation of hermetic and neoplatonic texts, studying Ptolemy's *Tetrabiblos and Centiloquium*, reading the works of Arab writers, including Abu Ma'shar, Al'Kindi and Averroes, the work known as the *Picatrix*, which had already been translated into Latin, and many others.

Yet in 1477 Ficino wrote the *Disputatio contra Iudicium Astrologorum*, (Against the Opinion of Astrologers), a substantial treatise several hundred pages in length, in which he attacked a large number of astrological practices. This text was never completed, nor published, but parts of it were incorporated into his letters and other works. When writing to Francesco Ippoliti, Count of Gazzoldo, he says 'I have written a book opposing the empty pronouncements of the astrologers. I am sending you the preface, and will send you the rest as our scribe has copied it.'[2]

In the *Disputatio*, Ficino condemned astrologers who asserted a person's mind and actions were moved by astral forces. He also disputed those partisans of fate when they declared that every event arose from a determinate cause in the heavens, and that once the planets had reached a particular position and configuration, a specific effect would inevitably follow.

Later, in 1489, he published the *De Vita Libri Tres* (Three Books on Life) in which he appears to contradict some of the views expressed in his earlier treatise, by endorsing astral causation when writing about astrological medicine. Hence he becomes, or sounds deterministic. If herbs infused with the spirit of, say, Jupiter, can cure an allergy in a person, then that would imply Ficino's acceptance that other powers of this planet can also affect us in other ways. Behind this apparent inconsistency lies the fundamental issue of man's freewill and to what extent celestial forces have dominion over human beings. This issue was extensively addressed by Ficino in the *Disputatio*, and further arguments appear in the *De Vita*.

Throughout his life, Ficino stressed the fundamental unity of the cosmos. In the *Disputatio* he states, 'Just as individual orders of things can be traced back to one single cause, all heat to absolute heat, all brightness to one supreme light, so the entire order of things is led back to one universal beginning and end of all; otherwise there would be no intrinsic unity in the world, no harmony between parts of the universe, finally no order...There is no lack of the good for any creature which can be conceived of; undoubtedly goodness is infinite, life everlasting, intellect utterly perfect, the will blessed...The immeasurable Godhead fills all everywhere just as infinite goodness extends itself through infinite space.'

Later on in the *Disputatio*, Ficino repeats a concept from *prisca theologia* about the cosmos being composed of distinct, hierarchically arranged realms ascending from physical matter, living beings which are ever changing, the subtle world of the mind/intellect – that is the rational soul which is indivisible but in some way changeable. The fourth level is occupied by the heavenly spheres whose influence is fixed. The highest level is the good itself, which is not only indivisible and immutable, but the absolute actuality and measureless.

Ficino goes on to state that the rational soul occupies the middle ground between eternity and time, being able to comprehend the lower worlds, receive illuminations from the celestial world and by the light of reason to choose freely between them. Quoting Plotinus and others, he argues that 'The movement of the heavenly bodies, the planets, are not the causes of inferior movements but rather instruments acting in compliance with divine movers, like artisans, whose multifarious thoughts foretelling the future are indicated to us by celestial bodies, figures, and movements.' (That is, indicated by the planets, their transits through twelve signs and aspects to each other.)

He strongly disagreed with those astrologers who declared that every single thing is necessarily brought to pass by the stars.[3] To ascribe causes of events to the celestial forces took away from God his own providence and absolute sovereignty over the universe. Furthermore, it denied men their freewill. He wrote 'Whoever says that wisdom and understanding are impelled by the stars, whose nature is fixed and prescribed, will remove the very reason itself of counsel which displays itself in spacious movement, unfettered and free on all sides; and in place of counsel will substitute a kind of narrow impulse.'[4] In Ficino's view, for man to act from freedom of choice is more noble than to act out of compulsion or necessity of nature, because above nature, intellect is master of his actions. It measures them, prescribes an end to each action and diversifies them, so that they are not necessarily the same, as in habitual actions, but appropriate to the moment.

The nature of the intellect also allows it to occupy itself with concepts concerning universal causes and to apply them in some particular action using the faculty of judgement. It is the discriminative intellect in man that gives him the freedom of choice, and distinguishes him from animals that have the faculty of judgement, but one that is pre-determined: like sheep that regard the wolf as being dangerous to them and flee on sight.

The implication of Ficino's statements on freewill is that man has been given the intellect to enable him to rise above the mechanical forces and outcomes *indicated*, but not caused, by the planets. The celestial powers affect the material realm, and to the extent our mind identifies with this realm, it comes under the dominion of the heavens. But, at any time man can act freely, then lives freely, and is not subject to any particular good or bad impulse from the celestial realm.

Ficino spelt out this fundamental concept in a letter to Francesco Marescalchi of Ferrara, written around the time that parts of the *Disputatio* were circulated by him. 'But perhaps someone may say it is foolish to wish to contend against unassailable fate. I, however, reply that it can be opposed as easily as one may wish to oppose it, since by that very opposition one may immediately overcome what one wishes. Surely the movement of the heavenly spheres is never able to raise the mind to a level higher than the spheres. But he who puts them under examination seems already to have transcended them, to have come near to God Himself and the free decision of the will.'[5]

Knowledge of astrology, and of the nature of planetary movements can remind a man that he is the witness of the celestial forces. Thus, transcending the limitations of their influences, he is one with the eternal, the good itself. As Shakespeare put it in *Julius Caesar*: 'Men at some time are masters of their fates: The fault, dear Brutus, is not in the stars, but in ourselves that we are underlings.'

Ficino, himself, did not find it easy to rise above the apparent forces of the planets, when he wrote to his close friend Giovanni Cavalcanti 'Saturn seems to have impressed a seal of melancholy on me from the beginning; set, as it is, almost in the midst of my ascendant in Aquarius, it is influenced by Mars, also in Aquarius, and the Moon in Capricorn.'[6]

Both Aquarius and Capricorn are, according to astrologers, ruled by Saturn denoting sorrow and restraint. But, Ficino also reminds his friend that one should praise Saturn, and all things should be given back to God, especially as on account of His gifts, denoted by Saturn, he had very little desire for worldly goods; thus leaving him free to pursue philosophy and nurture his flock in Florence.

Man's ability to transcend the celestial influences is given as advice to Lorenzo de' Medici, the Younger, when Ficino wrote 'Free-born Lorenzo; far greater than the heavens is He who made you; and you yourself will be far greater than the heavens as soon as you resolve upon the task. For these celestial bodies are not to be sought by us outside in some other place; for the heavens in their entirety are within us, in whom the light of life and the origin of heaven dwell.'[7] This statement also acknowledged a fundamental astrological principle that the human being is entirely composed of universal forces from basic physical elements, the celestial spheres, to the good itself.

In the same letter Ficino sets out the basic nature of the heavenly forces:

Moon signifies the continuous movement of our minds and body
Mars signifies swiftness and vigour
Saturn indicates our tardiness
Sun signifies God within us
Jupiter relates to laws divine and human
Mercury is counsel, reason, knowledge and discernment
Venus is our human nature whose soul and spirit are love and kinship

Each person receives in this life a portion of prosperity destined by fate from the stars outside us; and a portion of happiness freely available from the stars within us.[8] These are provided to us according to our virtues which would be based on the nature of our past and present actions.

On prophesying, Ficino states in the *Disputatio* that the future is not an ascertainable truth. So in this regard, astrology is not a science. Science is concerned with things that can be measured, are universal, everlasting and have fixed and ascertainable effects. Prognostication is difficult because knowledge of past events and previous experiences cannot be used as a guide. Predictions require knowledge of astrological principles, a natural aptitude combined with divine inspiration. To be a complete astrologer requires the ability to transcend the limits of mechanical rules and a wavering mind, in order to connect with the causal world beyond the spheres.

Ficino also dismissed predictions based on an examination of the heavenly bodies and observation of parents, the substance and customs of the local geographical region, and other inferior matters. He was scathing in his denunciation of astrologers who issued general prognostications on a daily basis such as we see today in nearly every newspaper and magazine, and those who professed divination, yet appeared to live and die according to chance.[9]

At no point in this substantial work did Ficino attack, or denounce, astrology itself. Only its application, the misguided beliefs and conduct of the professed astrologers of his day, came under attack from his pen. For Ficino continued to write and apply his skills on this subject throughout his life.

In the third book of the *De Vita* written in 1489, Ficino makes some extraordinary statements when one considers his previous pronouncements. There he shows how man may use his intellect to manipulate the cosmic forces by using the most propitious conditions and the universal powers to aid his activities. This book is entitled *De Vita coelitus comparanda* – (On obtaining life from the heavens). In the Proem addressed to the reader of this book, Ficino sets out his purpose for writing this part of the *De Vita*: 'The whole forms an epitome of medicine which will assist your life as much as possible, that it may be both healthy and long; and it employs at every point resources of doctors, aided by the heavens.'

The use of astrology to support medical diagnosis and to prescribe cures was generally accepted by 15th century society. Nevertheless Ficino was on delicate ground, as he acknowledged in three letters addressed to some of his closest friends, especially as the third book set out how to use magic and images. He supported his use of such forces by referring to Pythagoras and others who used their knowledge of the motions and influences of the heavens to obtain life and happiness for themselves and others.

The book sets out the means by which the desirable objectives of a long and healthy life may be obtained. 'If you want your body and spirit to receive power from some member of the cosmos, say from the Sun, seek the things which above all are most solar among metals and gems, still more among plants, and more yet among animals, especially human beings; for surely things which are more similar to you confer more of it. These must be brought to bear externally and, so far as possible, taken internally, especially in the day and hour of the Sun and while the Sun is dominant in a theme of the heavens.' He then goes on to explain which articles are solar, and which things belong to each of the other planets.

For instance, Jupiter rules articles such as silver, topaz, coral, sapphire, green and airy colours, wine, sugar, white honey, solemn music; and thoughts and feelings especially Jovial are steadfast, composed, religious, and law-abiding; and one should keep company with men of the same kind.

The principles enunciated by Ficino are not dissimilar to those of modern professional astrologers, particularly those in the Hindu Vedic tradition. Astrology would be a useless practice if clients were not able to receive guidance on how to overcome weaknesses and malign aspects in their life indicated, or confirmed, by the natal chart. So it is common practice for these astrologers to recommend a remedial measure, such as gemstones, precious metals and images, which are mentioned in the *De Vita*, to help their clients. According to Ficino, the purpose of such practices is to help people live a long and happylife.

In the *De Vita*, Ficino also sets out careers and other activities that accord with our mind and spirit which are signified by each planet giving similar affect, quality and pursuit. Jupiter's influence extends to civic occupations, such as law, religion, philosophy and those which strive for honour; Mars covers anger and contests; the Sun and Mercury, the pursuit of eloquence, of song, of truth, and of glory, and by skill; Venus, gaiety and music; Moon, a vegetable existence; and Saturn, withdrawal from human affairs, agriculture, theology, the more esoteric philosophy, and magic.

In choosing one main occupation in life Ficino offers the following advice: 'The specific rule for the individual would be to investigate which star promised what good to the individual at his nativity, to beg grace from that star rather than from another, and to await from any given star not just any gift and what belongs to other stars, but a gift proper to that one.'

Ficino states that no one should be in any doubt about our capacity to lay claim to celestial things by making certain preparations. 'For these lower things were made by the heavens, are continually ruled by them for our use.' In the *De Vita* there are many examples of how to use the planetary powers for our benefit. For instance, to take up a career that has a solar nature, a gemstone appropriate for the Sun should be worn. On the first occasion, this should be put on during the day and hour of the Sun – for the time of commencement is important – so that the celestial powers contained in the Sun will be passed down to our body and intellect.

In the *De Vita*, can be found information on medicines using herbs related to specific planets that when made at the right time can receive the appropriate celestial influences more easily. In this book, he appears to anticipate Nicholas Culpeper (1616 - 1654) in his *Complete Herbal*.

The *De Vita* is one of the few works on Ficino that details some of his knowledge of astrological principles. For instance, he gives information on planetary rulerships over the constellations and over different parts of the body. Also, he sets out in some depth the use of astronomical images in medicine, that are to be found in relatively obscure treatises. One example, according to Arabic texts, is the use of the figure of the cross as it is an ideal receptacle for the strength of the stars.

Towards the end of this book, Ficino anticipates condemnation from the Church that his work, extolling the use of celestial forces for our own good, will detract from our freewill, and derogate from the worship of the one God. Ficino's answer is simple and direct: 'Freedom of will is not repressed by the election of an excellent hour; rather, to scorn to elect an hour for the beginnings of great enterprises is not freedom but reckless choice.'

In a letter written in 1490 to Pierfilippo Pandolfini who was speaker of the Florentine Senate, Ficino quotes Ptolemy who declared 'The wise man acts in accordance with the operation of the stars, just as the farmer assists nature in cultivating the earth.'[10] Ficino is challenging the use of our intellect when we ignore the guiding spirit and knowledge available from the celestials that indicate the propitious time to commence any activity.

The same letter contains an example of Ficino being fully aware of the planetary daily movements. He used this knowledge to notify his friend of auspicious, and inauspicious, times for action on a daily basis for the forthcoming year, and advised him that when, in particular, Jupiter was in Gemini 'he should act whilst the fates are on his side'.

There is also a record of Ficino, together with other astrologers, being consulted by Filippo Strozzi as to the right time and place for laying the foundation stone of the Strozzi Palace that can still be seen today in Florence.[11] Electing a propitious time for such a beginning was relatively common in the 15th century, but Ficino regarded it as a mundane use of his talents.

As a result of studying the planetary movements for the present and future times, Ficino could foresee the dark clouds moving over Florence and the rest of Italy. He was so concerned, along with three other astrologers, about the fate of Italy, that they wrote the joint letter to Pope Sixtus, from which a small section is quoted at the beginning of this chapter. The letter also foretold that 'Many leaders from every nation will be overthrown, and then a new heresy under a false prophet will arise.' All these prophecies came about.[12]

In an earlier letter to Pope Sixtus written soon after the outbreak of war between Rome and Florence probably in the autumn 1478, Ficino advises the Pope to free himself from the bad influences of his lower nature indicated by an aggressive Mars and an unyielding Saturn in his natal chart. Instead he should allow Jupiter's magnanimity in his chart to establish love, peace, and law within his domain.[13] In 1480, a Turkish army landed at Otranto in Southern Italy, causing Sixtus to reach a quick settlement with Florence. The Jupiter side of his nature came through in his founding of hospitals, and patronising the arts which included building the Sistine Chapel.

In his writings, Ficino makes frequent use of the imagery of astrology primarily to raise his readers' minds to the heavens, and then to God, the source of all light and life. In a letter addressed to philosophers and teachers of sophistry he states 'The sun in the heavens gives birth to the eyes in creatures and the colours in objects, and the same sun shows those colours to eyes which are open and pure. The sun which is above the heavens, that is truth itself, is father both of minds and of true things.'[14]

Ficino believed that through astrology men could come to an understanding of the divine mind leading to a knowledge of themselves and of God. This is one of the themes in a book on the Sun, the *De Sole*, published in 1494, five years before his death. In the *De Sole*, Ficino starts with an explanation addressed to the reader that this book is allegorical and anagogical rather than dogmatic. He goes on to set out a number of basic mediaeval astrological principles, which demonstrate the Sun's dominion over the celestial forces. It is clear from these chapters that Ficino approved of judicious astrology, which uses the planetary positions at the time of birth and their subsequent movements in relation to the natal chart, as a basis for ascertaining individuals' destiny. He also set out the horoscope technique for judging 'the yearly fortune of the whole world' derived from the charts for equinoxes and solstices. These times are related to the Sun reaching particular cardinal points as it traverses the heavens, as viewed from the Earth. Ficino wrote 'Similarly, when the Sun returns by the exact degree and minute to its place in the nativity of any person, his share of the fortune, good or bad, is unfolded for the whole year.'

The last part of the *De Sole* is concerned with the two lights of the

Sun: the light of the corporeal Sun that prevails over the whole visible universe, and an incorporeal Sun presiding over the divine intellect. 'Plato called this light truth with respect to intelligible things and knowledge with respect to the minds of men.' The former relies on sensory perception, whilst the latter requires the intuitive faculty. This is the allegorical part of the book. Ficino reminds us that the Sun is not to be worshipped as the author of all things, for beyond the Sun is its cause, God. Nevertheless, men have access to these two lights through use of their intellect. The one can give them dominion over the visible world, the other access to the subtle world of the mind and beyond, through stillness and knowledge, to God.

The *De Sole* is profoundly different from the *De Vita* in which Ficino expounds other astrological techniques, especially those to be used for medical purposes. It brings together his religious and philosophical beliefs with his astrological ideas, and stresses the importance of the intuitive power of man which, according to the *Disputatio*, has to be used by astrologers if they were to divine the future from a chart of the planetary positions.

Ficino's astrological writings contain advice, not only for the Pope and leading men of his time, but for mankind for all times. He challenges our ideas about freewill, when he says that to ignore the indications of the stars is not exercising our freewill but ignorance. He constantly attempts to raise people's minds from the limited individual view to the universal level by use of astrological imagery and by reminding us that all the celestial universal powers without, are within each one of us. It is clear from his correspondence and treatises, that astrology for him requires the greatest use of man's intellectual and intuitive powers. Its purpose is to help everyone to be happy and live in accordance with their natural abilities and disposition by shedding light on those things about us which can remain hidden.

'Finally, to sum up' as he wrote to Lorenzo de Medici, the Younger, 'if by this reasoning you prudently temper within yourself the heavenly signs and the heavenly gifts, you will flee far from all the menaces of the fates and without doubt will live a blessed life under divine auspices.'[15]

NOTES

1. *The Letters of Marsilio Ficino*, 2, 10.
2. *Letters*, 3, 37.
3. *Letters*, 4, 37.
4. *Disputatio contra iudicium astrologorum.*
5. *Letters*, 3, 29.
6. *Letters*, 2, 24.
7. *Letters*, 4, 46.
8. *Letters*, 4, 47.
9. *Letters*, 3, 37.
10. Unpublished letter from Ficino, *Opera Omnis*, p. 918
11. Lorenzo Strozzi, in his *Vita di Filippo Strozzi*; 70
12. *Letters*, 5, 9, notes 6 and 8.
13. *Letters*, 5, 1. (Sixtus' natal chart is on page 120).
14. *Letters*, 4, 7.
15. *Letters*, 4, 46.

Ficino and Portraiture

PAMELA TUDOR-CRAIG

"I have often looked for myself...I have gazed at this face
in the mirror...but I could never say I have...seen myself.
For when I seek myself, it is exactly the same Marsilio that
is both seeker and sought...it is spirit alone I seek, since I
seek myself, who am indeed pure spirit... *

AND there lies, in a nutshell, the essential difference between Italian and Northern European portraiture in the second half of the fifteenth century. Despite the magisterial volume by Lorne Campbell[1] in which, by dealing with topics that cross the boundaries between north and south, and by emphasising common concerns of practical importance to the portrait painter, in some measure he blurs the distinction, it still holds. The Flemish, or the French portrait of Ficino's working lifetime presented the particular, without fear or flattery, and was admired for its detailed veracity. Its Italian counterpart, for all that it was equally capable of catching a speaking likeness, attempted to go beyond that, as Ficino went beyond it in gazing at his mirror image. In Italy it was required of the artist to suggest, in addition to the appearance of the sitter, those less tangible qualities of character, and even, maybe, in works of genius, a spiritual dimension.

In *De Viris Illustribus* written in 1456 when Ficino was 23, Bartolommeo Fazio defined the aim as representation: '...not only of the face or countenance and the lineaments of the whole body but also, and far more, of its interior feelings and emotions...' His source was the Greek Philostratus who gave as the foundation of art the ability to

---

* Ficino, *Letters*, Vol 1, letter 38, to Giovanni Cavalcanti

101

'distinguish... the signs of men's character... whatever has to do with the mind...'[2]

Both traditions sprang immediately from the introduction into pictures of religious subjects of the representation, from the fourteenth century increasingly the recognisable representation,[3] of the donor. Realistic portraiture had not been a serious option in the centuries of generalisation between classical times and the fourteenth century. Now, in all western Europe, from the profile of Jean II in the Louvre and the gilt bronze of Edward III in Westminster Abbey, we find ourselves encountering real people. Nor did that privilege stay for more than one generation the exclusive perogative of royalty. However, more often than we immediately recognise, the isolated bust length panel portrait of a Flemish bourgeois gentleman was once part of a diptych, paired with a devotional picture of Christ, or more probably of the Virgin and Child.[4] A three-quarter view, with the sitter or sitters in rapt attention, sometimes with hands raised in prayer, proclaims the intended counterpart. The drive, on the part of Roger van den Weyden or Hans Memling, was to achieve the most perfect verisimilitude in order to capture the person at the intersection of Time and Eternity. The person represented Time, the icon Eternity. In this context portraiture retained something of its original inferior status as a marginal donor figure. In Van Eyck's day the head had reached the dignity of representation on the same scale as holy figures, but there was a lingering trace of diminution in the portrayal of the hands.

If Northern portraiture grew naturally from the donor, politely introduced by their patron saint, in the corner of painted panel or illumination, Italian portraits owed more to the rediscovery of the classical sculpted portrait bust, and to classical coinage. Already Pisanello had drawn heavily upon coins for his famous medal gallery begun in the later 1430's. A decade later Andrea Mantegna attracted his first recorded praise for a portrait of a nun 'of an angelic face beneath a veil...sculpted in paint...'[5] 'Sculpted in Paint' declares the recognition of Mantegna's archaeological sources. To convey the illusion of living features seen through a veil has been one of the perennial challenges to the sculptor. The enduring influence over

Mantegna of classical sculpture invested the brutal features of Cardinal Ludovico Trevisan, whom he painted in 1459-60,[6] with Imperial dignity. It would seem that concentration on the likeness was one respect in which the Roman Empire had extended the range of Greek sculpture. That concentration had been in response to a double demand. The actual appearance of the ruler had to be well known across his Empire, to avoid spurious impersonations. And it had to inspire awe, for his image was required to receive worship. The various and sometimes unpromising features of the actual Emperors were clothed in the attributes of dignity, long-sightedness, power or intelligence. The Classical capacity to delineate 'whatever has to do with the mind', as Philostratus put it, were inherited by the Italian painters of Ficino's generation.

The two most remarkable expositions of Italian mastery of portraiture are both fresco schemes carried out in Ficino's younger years. Mantegna's *Camera Picta* of 1465-74 in the Palazzo Ducale in Mantua may have had as its occasion the elevation of a member of the Gonzaga family to the Cardinalate, but it is a profoundly secular (and original) celebration of the glory of a dynasty. The earlier transformation of an entire room into a dynastic celebration is Benozzo Gozzoli's Medici Chapel in the Palazzo Medici in Florence. No doubt if we had been living in Florence at the time we would have recognised every participant in this Adoration of the Magi. It is too easy to be dazzled by its resplendent pageantry, and to forget that all here serves a deeply religious purpose. Three generations of the Medici, with their entourage and distinguished visitors, are caught up in pilgrimage to the Heavenly Jerusalem, lovingly and engagingly represented in the tiny chancel. All are focussed upon the touching panel painting of the Christ Child as the Word of God, worshipped by his kneeling Mother and by the Baptist. This is perhaps the most popular subject of Florentine art, from Gentile da Fabriano to Filippino Lippi. It is easy enough to point out how well the theme chimed with contemporary love of pageantry, and what a splendid 'photo opportunity' it gave for a wealthy society to pose in their most wonderful brocades. What it is particularly important to remember is that this scene was acted out annually through the Florentine streets, in a Procession of the Magi that wended its way past this Palace to San Marco. No wonder Cosimo de'Medici asked the same artist to paint him as the Old King in another representation of the same subject in the Cell reserved for his own use in that monastery. The Medici themselves participated in this Act of Devotion.

So it is possible to contrast in general Flemish and Northern European portraiture, where the likeness may be created to continue, like a candle lit beside a devotional object, the prayer life of the person, and Italian portraiture of Ficino's time, which also aimed to convey the interior life of the sitter. However, we can see in the Medici Chapel itself, painted when Ficino was young, that the interior (Italian) and exterior (Flemish) aspects, the meditation and the external observance, might be fused. After all, in 1473 Ficino himself became a Priest. Clearly he felt the need not only for his own internal search for Himself, but for the acting out of that search in terms of the rituals of the Church. His mirror reflected the man aware of his immortal spirit, and also of its destination beyond his present self.

NOTES

1. Lorne Campbell, *Renaissance Portraits,* Yale University Press, New Haven and London, 1990.

2. Keith Christiansen in the chapter 'Portraits' in Jane Martineau, (ed.) *Andrea Mantegna*, Royal Academy of Arts, London and Metropolitan Museum of Arts, New York, 1992 pp.324-48 esp.p.325.

3. A natural starting point would be the profile portrait of Robert, his younger brother, kneeling in supplication at the feet of the seated St. Louis of Toulouse by Simone Martini, 1317, in the Museo de Capodimonte in Naples. Only accuracy could excuse so plain a face.

4. See Angelica Duhlberg: *Privat Porträts: Geschichte und Ikonologie einer Gattung in 15 und 16 Jahrhundert*, Berlin,1990. See for example no. 51, Hans Memling, Madonna and Child, Luton Hoo, Wernher Coll., cat.146 and portrait of Gilles Joye, 1472, Williamstown Mass., Stirling and Francis Clark Art Institute, also Cat. 146. See also no.52, Roger van der Weyden, Madonna and

Child, 145055, cat. 154 in Tournai, Musée des Beaux Arts, and portrait of Jean de Gras, same date, Art Institute of Chicago, again cat. 154. Here Duhlberg has reunited two pairs of parted diptychs. In each case the portrait has gone to the United States.

5. Christiansen, *op. cit.* p.324. Of the appearance of Ficino himself there are modest initial illuminations in manuscripts of his works, which accord with the posthumous fresco in the Palazzo Pitti in Florence where he appears among his Academy, and the fine sculpted half-length memorial in Florence Cathedral. He is probably one of the group taken from the life known as the Four Philosophers in the scene of Zachariah in the Temple, part of Domenico Ghirlandaio's fresco cycle of before 1490 in Sta.Maria Novella. The bust is illustrated as the frontispiece to *The Letters*, *op.cit.*,vol.1. It is clear that Ficino was not interested in these incidentals.

6. *op. cit.* pp.333-4 illus., cat. 100.

Dean Colet

JENIFER CAPPER

The eternal alone is true, the temporal only seems to be. *

WITHIN the context of this essay, I will not attempt to give a detailed analysis of the relationship between Dean Colet and Marsilio Ficino, but rather to consider the nature of their friendship, in the context of the society in which they were living and the changes which were taking place. To give a little insight into the character of John Colet, I quote from the following letter:

> When you have read the contents of this letter, please to let me have it back again, as I have not a copy of it by me. And though I am not in the habit of keeping my letters by me (nor could I do so, because they are sent off by me as first written, without any copy being retained,) still, if there are any which contain matters of doctrine, I should not like them to be altogether lost. Not that they are worth preservation; but if left behind they might help to keep alive some recollection of me. And whatever other reason there may be for my wishing the letters I write to you to be preserved, this one is certainly the strongest, that I should like them to remain as enduring witness of my respect for you. Again farewell.[1]

The aim of John Colet's life was to follow God's will and come to a greater understanding of his will through the teachings of Christ. Therefore he made no effort to preserve anything personal and consequently very little is known about his life. The little which does

* Ficino, *Letters*, Vol 3, letter 19

survive, is piecemeal and fragmentary which means that conclusions would be questionable. However, thanks to many quotations from Erasmus, who held Colet in very high regard, and to his achievements as the founder of St. Paul's School for Boys, plus his lecture notes on various books of the *Bible* and such correspondence as has been found, it is possible to gain some insight into the life and achievements of John Colet.

To come to any understanding on this subject however, it is important that they are evaluated in the context of their times. For the period when John Colet (1467 - 1519) and Marsilio Ficino (1433 - 1499) were living, was to see very radical changes, which were to have a profound influence not only on their lives, but on the generations which were to follow for at least the next five hundred years. It would not be too exaggerated to say that both these men played a major part in shaping the way in which these changes took place.

The body of the Church was to undergo a vast Reformation, and since Ficino and John Colet were both clerics, it had a very direct impact upon their lives, as it did on the lives of all. The most powerful body in England at this time was undoubtedly the Roman Catholic Church. In many ways it is difficult for us to imagine what this influence was. There was only the One Universal Catholic Church. The teachings of the Catholic Church were an integral part of every man's and woman's life. It held sway over Western Europe and the most terrible penalty it could exact on anyone who questioned its authority was excommunication. Today there is no requirement put upon anyone to believe in anything, unlike the Greeks and Romans who would have charged you with impiety if you did not subscribe to their idea of a world ruled by the Gods, a crime punishable by death, or in Tudor times, when you would have been regarded as a heretic if you did not conform and burnt at the stake. Therefore the idea of a community belonging exclusively to one religion whose moral life is ruled by the tenets laid down by this religion, is difficult for us to envisage. Since the Church had become rich and very powerful over the centuries and in fact at this time, owned a third of the land in England, it no longer confined itself to spiritual matters. For many, the Church was seen as a way of advancement particularly if you had not been born into the higher levels of society. Thomas Wolsey is a good example of this. He was a butcher's son and for a time enjoyed a very distinguished career which began as a cleric and ended as Lord Chancellor, which apart from the King, was the most powerful office. Inevitably this led to a great deal of corruption in the Church, but it continued to hold sway over people because it denied them the right to read the *Bible* for themselves and encouraged them to believe that the only hope for their salvation lay in the Church. Therefore they relied exclusively on the Church for their spiritual nourishment, as this body alone had access to the *Bible*. However, with the development of the printing press and the rise of the great Reformers, such as Martin Luther in Germany and John Wyclif in England, who produced pamphlets and started to question the authority of the Church, little by little the power of the Church began to lessen. It is important to realise that they did not question the fundamental teachings of Christ, but rather the interpretation of the Church, and they promoted the idea that the *Bible* should be made available to all.

What is interesting to note is the attitude of some of the leading Churchmen in England at this time. They themselves were very devout Catholics, but they realised times were changing.

What, my Lord, shall we build houses and provide livelihoods for a company of monks whose end and fall we may ourselves live to see? No, no; it is more meet a great deal that we should have care to provide for the increase of learning, and for such as by their learning shall do good to the Church and the commonwealth...'[2]

This refers to the practice which had been commonplace, of giving large sums to charity which had enabled the Church to become very wealthy. People gave their wealth to the Church in the belief that it would absolve them of their sins and secure a place in heaven for them, an idea assiduously promoted by the Church. Bishop Fox as a result, founded Corpus Christi College, Oxford, instead in 1515; and yet the major dissolution of the monasteries did not take place until

1536. Another example which is worth mentioning is that of Bishop Fisher, who was the confessor to Margaret Beaufort, the mother of Henry VII, a very devout Catholic. He lost his head in the reign of Henry VIII because he refused to accept the King as the Supreme Head of the Church. He advised Margaret Beaufort to leave her wealth to Cambridge University and the promotion of the printing press rather than endowing any more religious houses. Under his guidance, not only did her wealth give a great boost to the printing press, but she also founded the first chair of Greek at Cambridge which Erasmus was the first person to fill.

This brings us to the next major change in England where we see directly the work of both Marsilio Ficino and John Colet. As men no longer had confidence in the spirituality of the Church, where would they turn to unlock the mysteries of their faith? So they turned to the continent where a new movement had already began to spread, namely what we call the Renaissance. Speaking very broadly, this was made possible because the trade routes had opened up and therefore, there was much more communication of ideas between the countries. It was easier for people to travel and it was common for students to visit other great universities such as Paris, Florence, Orleans; and John Colet himself spent some time in Italy.

To add to this, they began to search for manuscripts in the different areas which both the Greeks and the Romans had occupied during their long history. This opened up a whole new world for them. There were treatises on every subject imaginable; and to add to this, the devoted work of those who copied these manuscripts out by hand, and the widespread development of the printing press, meant that these manuscripts were accessible to many more. An enthusiasm for learning and the desire to translate and have access to this knowledge was overwhelming. The study of Latin was not new, but Greek was almost unknown. This effort to study Greek was beset with great difficulties. Erasmus who occupied the first chair of Greek at Cambridge was not impressed by the calibre of the English students and it is a well known fact that many of them did not stay the course but escaped, it is said, by night, quite unable to meet the demands of their tutor. They approached scholarship in a very different way. They did not disseminate and critically analyse in the way in which we approach it today, but simply read and studied assiduously anything they could lay their hands on so that they might unlock the mysteries of the classical world. Their aim was fundamentally a religious one. They studied to enhance their understanding of their own religion, not to find a new religion.

To give some idea of just how comprehensive their study was, here is the basic curriculum of a University degree. When a student went up to Oxford to embark upon his degree in Divinity (there was no other degree except that of Divinity), he would embark upon the study of the Trivium and the Quadrivium which would take him eight years to complete. The Trivium, which was the elementary part of this education, occupied the first two years and was concerned with the expression of thought and eloquence. The disciplines studied were Grammar, Rhetoric and Logic. Having completed this, the student would then embark upon the contents of the Quadrivium which comprised Arithmetic for a year, Music for a year, two terms of Geometry, two terms of Astronomy, three terms of Natural Philosophy, three terms of Moral Philosophy and three terms of Metaphysics. The discipline of the Quadrivium was concerned with acquiring wisdom. John Colet was one of these young men who went up to Oxford for this purpose.

In the words of Erasmus:

> ...[Colet] diligently mastered all the philosophy of the schools, and gained the title expressive of a knowledge of the seven liberal arts. Of these arts there was not one in which he had not been industriously and successfully trained. For he had both eagerly devoured the works of Cicero, and diligently searched into those of Plato and Plotinus...[3]

It was at this point in his life that John Colet encountered Marsilio Ficino. For when he went to Oxford and took up the subjects prescribed by the Quadrivium, the philosophy which was part of the curriculum was Aristotle. However he became fascinated by the works of Plato and studied them in very great depth. Therefore, as he did not learn Greek until he was fifty, (1516), and as he was at Oxford probably between 1483 and 1499, spending four of those years on the continent, the only access he would have had to Plato would have been through Ficino's Latin translations of Plato's works. Ficino under the patronage of Cosimo de'Medici had not only translated the works of Plato from Greek to Latin, but had written commentaries on the different dialogues and had used his published correspondences with others to express Platonic thought. For John Colet, the works of Ficino enabled him to make a more thorough study of Plato than would otherwise have been possible. However, it is also worth mentioning that Colet did not rely on Ficino alone, but also investigated the work of Plotinus and Dionysius the Areopagite, who had both written expositions on the teachings of Plato. There is no doubt that the works of Plato had a profound effect upon Colet. Again, in the words of Erasmus:

When I hear Colet I seem to be listening to Plato himself. [4]

Perhaps it is appropriate at this point to consider the nature of the association between John Colet and Marsilio Ficino. Why should a man such as John Colet who was a devout Roman Catholic, with an unshakeable faith in his religion, have had a correspondence with Ficino who, although a cleric, had taken up the study of philosophy and was considered to be more of a humanist than a churchman? This is Colet's view of philosophers:

Those books alone ought to be read, in which Christ is set forth for us to feed upon. These books in which Christ is not found are but a table of devils. Do not become readers of philosophers, companions of devils. [5]

Yet he did have a correspondence and although cautious of philosophers, he does not appear to have regarded Plato or Ficino in the same light. Nevertheless it does still raise an interesting question. Why did a deeply religious man look outside his own religion? The scholar Sears Jayne, whose book *John Colet and Marsilio Ficino* provides a much more detailed analysis based on manuscript evidence of the connection between these two men, poses the question in this way,

Why does man constantly seek to confirm what he knows as if one authority is not enough? Why does he seek to find parallels in other religions and philosophical teachings?

To consider this question, I believe does give us some insight into what drew these two men together. To begin with, it would be useful at this point to consider this within the context of Colet's life. There were two major preoccupations in Colet's life: the commentaries which he wrote on the different books of the *Bible* particularly St. Paul, whom he considered to be the wisest of the Christian theologians and who was undoubtedly his hero. He made a life-long study of *Corinthians* and *Romans*. To add to this, he was a Churchman and was frequently required to give lectures and sermons, particularly at the court of Henry VIII. His other major interest was education which led to the founding of St. Paul's School. In the context of his role as a Churchman and the need to give lectures and sermons, he found in the works of Plato and the commentaries of Ficino a way of enhancing his own understanding of the gospels. This also provided inspiration for him and enabled him to transmit in a more convincing way the argument which he wished to convey. It confirmed what he ardently believed and gave him the logical principles he needed to explain these beliefs. This essay does not provide the scope to elaborate upon this point and there are scholars who have looked into this in much greater depth. Nevertheless it would be appropriate to mention two areas: one was undoubtedly a much more detailed description of the ascent and descent of the soul which is not given in detail by the Christian teachings. Equally the position of the angels, archangels and daemons is treated in a more comprehensive manner within Platonic thought than in Christian theology.

Here are excerpts from Colet, Ficino and Plato which I hope will illuminate one of the subjects I mentioned, namely the ascent and descent of the soul.

Colet:

When the Spirit is taken away, there is a change of form in all things, not least in the Church and beauty is turned into deformity. But if the Spirit of God be present with the Church, then from His essence, which is one with the Father and Church, there flows a spiritual being into all members of the Church. By this influx they are in the first place begotten again to a spiritual being, and in the next are sustained therein. Thus the act of that essence of God in us is our spiritual being in Him. For the act of essence is being. And just as from the Spirit's essence there flows unity and spiritual being into the several members of the Church, so from the power of the same essence there flows a spiritual working in every spiritual man, accompanying his spiritual being.[6]

Colet then adds in his expositions on *Romans* his concept of Truth:

The separate existence of Truth as a set of absolute and unchanging principles known in its entirety only to God and known to man only to the extent that God had revealed it. All knowledge of Truth is from revelation and there are only so many authorities whom God has used for that purpose.[7]

Ficino:

The soul is at first in the presence of God, where it is satisfied and happy. Then, because of its desire for and love of the body, it falls into the body and is united with it. There, like a person drowning in a stormy sea, the soul is overcome by oblivion, the lack of knowledge (of heaven) whence all evils spring... but the soul easily passes out of the dense shadows into a remembrance of truer things. At length it recalls its own nature, and, recognising and despising the meanness of the body, it seeks to return to its natural home (ie. heaven) and feed once more on nectar and ambrosia, that is, the vision of Truth, and to rejoice in the possession of the Good. It discovers and beats its wings; it comes to life again in its dead body; it is awakened from sleep; it emerges from the river Lethe and, stretching its long unused (wings of) goodness and wisdom, tries to fly back to heaven.[8]

Plato:

But when (the soul) returning into herself she reflects, then she passes into the other world, the region of purity, and eternity, and immortality, and unchangeableness, which are her kindred, and with them she ever lives, when she is by herself and is not let or hindered; then she ceases from her erring ways, and being in communion with the unchanging is unchanging. And this state of the soul is called wisdom.[9]

Colet believed that the only way to attain to this revelation or essence, was through purification, illumination and perfection, which he had taken from Dionysius' description of the ascent of the soul.In relation to the two quotations from Ficino and Plato, I have put them one after the other because Ficino is describing how the soul, having moved out of the corporeal region in search of heaven, may then feed on the vision of Truth, while Plato gives us the culmination of this ascent by his description of the true state of Wisdom. By offering these three quotations, I am not attempting to make any comparison, but rather to highlight the similarity in their approach to perhaps the most important aim in life, namely the quest for the Truth. They all stand on common ground in that they all acknowledge that real understanding can only be found in revelation. For this process requires us to put aside the whole world of concepts and ideas and move into the solitude of the soul standing alone by itself, which is the very contemplation of the Truth, to use the words of Plato, and only then can the Truth be revealed. You may well ask then, why bother to study? Again I will turn to the words of Ficino who resolves this conundrum.

Paul and Dionysius, the wisest of the Christian theologians, affirm that the invisible things of God are understood from what has been made and is to be seen here, but (and) Plato says that the wisdom of men is the image of divine wisdom.... Thus when the soul has received through the physical senses those images which are within material objects, we remember what we knew before when we existed outside the prison of the body. The soul is fired by this memory and, shaking its wings, by degrees it purges itself from contact with the body and its filth and becomes wholly possessed by divine frenzy.[10]

To underline this point further: namely 'when the soul has received through the physical senses those images which are within the material objects...'

This leads us to another major topic which influenced not only Colet's approach to his religious duties but his aims in establishing his school. For like Socrates and Plato, John Colet believed the world of the senses should be avoided at all costs, as it dragged the soul downwards; using the words of Plato who believed that man's and woman's most important task in life was to avoid contact with the senses as far as possible, so that the soul might find refuge in the upper regions where it could contemplate and come to know its true nature. Here is an extract from a letter written by Erasmus to Justus Jonas, describing life in the deanery of St. Paul's:

The dean's table, which in former days had ministered to luxury under the guise of hospitality, he brought within the bounds of moderation. For, having done without suppers entirely for some years before, he was thus free from company in the evening. Moreover as he dined rather late, he had fewer guests on those occasions as well; and all the fewer because the repast, though neat, was frugal, and the sitting at table short, and, lastly, the conversation such as to have no charms but for the good and learned. When grace had been said, a boy would read aloud, in a clear distinct voice, a chapter from St. Paul's *Epistles*, or from the *Proverbs* of Solomon. He would then usually repeat some passage selected from the part read, and draw a subject of conversation from it, inquiring of any scholars present, or even of intelligent laymen, what this or that expression meant. And he would so season the discourse that, though both serious and religious, it had nothing tedious or affected about it. Again towards the end of the meal, when the requirements of nature, at any rate, if not of pleasure, had been satisfied, he would start some other topic; and thus bade farewell to his guests, refreshed in mind as well as in body, and better men at leaving than they came, though with stomachs not overloaded.[11]

The reason for quoting this story is to point to the far reaching changes which were taking place throughout the European community from the grotesque wealth and reliance upon it which had dominated the Church for so many centuries, and the desire to simplify life and live in purity which they believed was the only way in which a person might move closer to communion with God. In Colet's private life he lived very austerely and encouraged a very frugal way of life. Again the similarity in approach is evident.

This same principle runs through the structure of the curriculum which he created for the boys of St. Paul's school, and cannot but remind everyone of the principles laid down by Plato for the education of young children in his ideal state, which he spells out in the *Republic*. To do justice to this subject would require a whole work in itself, so forgive me if I select only a few salient points within this context. The first principle to consider is why he felt it necessary to establish this foundation:

> ...Colet's intention in founding the school is to increase the knowledge and worship of God.[12]

Equally in Colet's statutes we discover the requirements he lays down for the selection of the High Master which reflect a similar sound:

> ...a man hoole in body honeste and vertuouse and learnyed in good and clene laten literature and also in greke yf suche may be gotten...[13]

In laying down the curriculum for his school it is very obvious that Colet believed it was necessary to maintain the purity of the children, to fulfil his ultimate aim, namely to increase the knowledge and worship of God. Therefore the material used was carefully vetted. Let us turn to Plato:

> ...and all the battles of the gods in Homer – these tales must not be admitted into our state, whether they are supposed to have

an allegorical meaning or not. For a young person cannot judge what is allegorical and what is literal; anything that he receives into his mind at that age is likely to become indelible and unalterable; and therefore it is most important that the tales which the young first hear should be models of virtuous thought.[14]

It is interesting to note that in the section of Colet's statutes which deal with what should be taught, not one of the six authors who are mentioned in that list belongs to the period of classical literature. Lactantius lived in the fourth century. Proba, who was his contemporary, compiled a work called *Centones Virgiliani* which was a poem he had composed using lines of Virgil taken out of context to make up A Life of Christ. Prudentius was known in the Middle Ages as the Christian Pindar. His *Psychomia* was used as a school book by Alcuin in the eighth century, by Bruno in the tenth century, and in the fifteenth century by Vives, the tutor at the court school to Princess Mary and also a fellow of Corpus Christi College Oxford. In the area of Greek, Colet did not specify certain authors which may well be due to his limited knowledge of Greek literature:

I wolde they were taught always in good literature both Latin and Greke.[15]

It is a well established fact that St. Paul's was the first public school to teach Greek. However he chose the material which was to be presented to the boys very carefully. The following quotation sums up Colet's view perfectly:

...I say that fylthynesse and all such abusyon which the later worlde brought in which more ratyr may be called blotterature thenne litterature I utterly abbanysh and Exclude oute of this scole.[16]

Likewise he set the same high standards for his selection of the High Master:

The master of the grammar school,' they provide, 'shall be a good and honest man, and of much and well attested learning. Let him teach the boys, especially those belonging to the cathedral, grammar, and at the same time show them an example of good living. Let him take great heed that he cause no offence to their tender minds by any pollution of word or deed. Nay, more, along with chaste literature let him imbue them with holy morals, and be to them a master, not of grammar only, but of virtue.[17]

Since we are looking at the foundation of the school, it is worth considering who these pupils were.

There shall be taught in the scole children of all nacions and countres indifferently to the noumber of a cliii accordyng to the Noumber of the Setys in the scole.[18]

This in itself was remarkable as it contained no restrictions and welcomed all, whatever their creed. However there were certain criteria which had to be fulfilled. Colet insisted on a knowledge of reading and writing and of the Catechism, as a condition for entry to the school and:

On entering the school every boy had to pay a fee of fourpence which went to the pore Scoler that swepith the scole.[19]

We know that beyond this, there was no other charge. However it does indicate that some charge was made although it was ostensibly to provide for those who couldn't afford the fourpence. Looking at the basic statutes of some of the other schools which were founded at this time, it is clear that some were exclusively for children who were poor, such as Charterhouse, Westminster and Merchant's Taylors.

This proved to be a remarkable period in the history of education. A middle class had arisen, loyal to the King because he had given them an opportunity of improving their situation. He needed them because he no longer relied exclusively on the aristocracy. Many of the middle class had become wealthy through trade, and they wanted to give their children the opportunity to have the benefits of a good education. Therefore they ploughed their wealth into education. The schools which had previously been the domain of the Church now looked to trade and industry. Both had now begun to create livery companies such as the Mercers and the Merchant Taylors, to name but two. Colet appointed the Mercers as governors of his new school. This quotation is taken from a letter of Erasmus:

Over the revenues and entire management, he set neither priests, nor the Bishop nor the chapter, but some married citizens of established reputation; and when asked the reason, he said that though there was nothing certain in human affairs, he yet found the least corruption in them.[20]

Another qualification which he put upon them was that the governors should be re-elected every two years, to avoid corruption setting in. Again, this is echoed in Plato's *Laws*, where he deals with the election of the different officers for the administration of the state. To avoid corruption, he suggests a fairly complex system for the actual election; and a time limit is placed on the period in office, including that of the guardian of the state, who may only rule for a maximum of twenty years. Both men understood the weakness of human nature and the need to protect human institutions from the inevitable corruption which inevitably sets in over a period of time. Thus in laying down his principles for education, Colet took great care to ensure that it would be protected.

What becomes very clear when reflecting on the life of John Colet is that this was a period in history which was full of potential as the fabric of the society was undergoing change. This can produce a state of uncertainty in any community and it is incumbent upon those who hold influential positions in their society to pursue their goals with integrity and for the benefit of the community as a whole. It was an extraordinary fact that at this time, there was a large group of men and women working together to create stability and order in the community. The two institutions upon which they focused were the Church and Education. Their efforts did finally help the community to connect once again with the essence of the teachings of Christ and to remain single minded despite the difficulties which were encountered through the process of its evolution until the Act of Settlement during the reign of Elizabeth 1. In Education a system was created which provided education for anyone who owned a pair of shoes and could therefore walk to school and was willing to come under the formidable discipline which was offered in these schools. It had also created a model, as with other schools of that time, which would be used as a system to instruct children for the next five hundred years. This gave order to an educational system which was dissolving because of the demise of the Church and paved the way for the communication between the schools and the Universities as they struggled to meet the demands for material which the Universities came to provide. As their aim was to increase the knowledge and the worship of God, their vision was trained on higher things and therefore they looked to the world of Spirit. This was made possible by the Ficino's translations and commentaries of Plato's dialogues.

The approach of these two men although quite different in that Colet was a devout Catholic seeking to penetrate the teachings of Christ as the ultimate path to Wisdom, whereas Ficino, although a cleric himself, looked to the philosophy of Plato and Hermes Trismegistos, nevertheless, both men understood what is perhaps the most important point of all which is that all authorities are simply the guides that provide the light along the path to understanding and that Revelation is known only to the extent that God has revealed it.

NOTES

1. John Colet to the Abbot of Winchcombe, JH Lupton *A Life of Dean Colet*, George Bell & Son, 1909
2. *Ibid.*
3. *Ibid.*
4. Sears Jayne, *John Colet and Marsilio Ficino,* Oxford University Press, 1963
5. JH Lupton, *A Life of Dean Colet*
6. *Ibid.*
7. Sears Jayne
8. *Ibid.*
9. *Phaedo* 74: B. Jowett: *The Dialogues of Plato*, Random House 1939
10. Sears Jayne

11. Lupton
12. McDonald, *A History of St. Paul's School*, Chapman and Hall, 1909
13. *Ibid.*
14. *Republic,* B. Jowett
15. McDonald
16. *Ibid.*
17. Lupton
18. McDonald
19. *Ibid.*
20. *Ibid.*

Ficino and Shakespeare

JILL LINE

*Some, who imitate the divine and heavenly harmony with
deeper and sounder judgment, render a sense of its inner
reason and knowledge into verse, feet and numbers. It is
these who, inspired by the divine spirit, give forth with full
voice the most solemn and glorious song.* *

BY 1599, a hundred years after the death of Ficino, Shakespeare was
well established as a popular dramatist. The general public flocked to
his plays in the Bankside theatres and his company was frequently
invited to entertain at court and in the great houses of the nobility,
where his poems were also admired. The universal and timeless appeal
of his plays has increased in popularity over the years until it has
grown into the huge Shakespeare industry that we know today. His
genius is undisputed and many would agree that he was indeed 'inspired
by the divine spirit,' but it is seldom acknowledged that the flowering
of Shakespeare's writing in the English Renaissance had its roots in
Ficino's philosophy of Christian-Platonism that had inspired the
Renaissance in Italy.

The many works of the leader of the Florentine Academy, including
his translations and commentaries, were contained in a number of
English libraries from as early as 1500 and his *De Amore*, which of
all his writings is reflected most constantly in Shakespeare's, became
well known in England when it was published in French by Guy le
Fevre de la Boderie in 1578. At this time Shakespeare was fourteen
years old, growing up into a society imbued with this knowledge. The
works of many other poets of the English Renaissance reflect the

*Ficino, *Letters,* Vol 1, letter 7, p.46

influence of Ficino, whilst the masques that Jonson and his designer, Inigo Jones, presented at the court of King James are steeped in Christian-Platonism. But all these were written for an educated elite, schooled to recognise veiled allusions to spiritual growth and unity. On the other hand, through his genius as a poet, Shakespeare transmuted these ideas into plays that delighted all audiences and that will continue to entertain, educate and inspire for all time.

Whilst Shakespeare's plays may be enjoyed and understood in myriads of ways, essentially they are allegories of either man's return to union with, or separation from, himself. In Ficino's *De Amore*, his commentary on Plato's *Symposium on Love* to which he gave the added dimension of Christianity, he explains how, through love, God creates the worlds of mind, soul, nature and body. These worlds are not only in the macrocosm but are within man himself (a term used throughout to include both men and women). Finding himself in this physical world, man has the opportunity to make the return journey towards unity with God, that is, the Platonic One who in the microcosm is his own self, by falling in love with the beauty of each world in the reverse order of creation:

... just as a single ray of the sun lights up four bodies, fire, air, water, and earth, so a single ray of God illuminates the Mind, the Soul, Nature and Matter. And just as anyone who sees the light in those four elements is looking at a ray of the sun itself and, through that ray is turned to looking at the supreme light of the sun, so anyone who looks at and loves the beauty in those four, Mind, Soul, Nature and Body, is looking at and loving the splendour of God in them and, through this splendour, God Himself.[1]

By placing his lovers on this path towards union with God, Shakespeare clearly had the same intention as Ficino, who hoped that his *De Amore* 'would summon the lost lovers of earthly beauty to return to the love of immortal beauty.'[2]

The lover suffers the first pangs of desire when he is attracted to the physical beauty of his beloved, who personifies love, beauty and his own soul. This beauty 'is a certain blossom of goodness, by the charms of which blossom, as by a kind of bait, the hidden internal goodness...'[3] and so, if his love (and his beloved) is virtuous and sincere, the lover learns through his own nature that outward charm is but a shadow of the beauty of virtue lying hidden within the soul. By loving its goodness and beauty, the lover now becomes one with his soul, a union that Shakespeare often symbolises by marriage. 'Moreover,' wrote Ficino, 'that light and beauty of the soul we comprehend with the Intellect alone.'[4] So, by becoming one with his soul, the lover can enter the world of the intellect or higher mind, that Ficino also calls the angelic world. When, in its turn, the beauty of intellect arouses his love, he is enabled to achieve union with the angelic world that moves towards 'its own apex or head before it ascends to God.'[5]

This Platonic concept of love lies at the heart, not only of the intrigues of lovers in Shakespeare's comedies and romances, but also, in some form or other, of all his plays. In truth, all Shakespeare's heroes are lovers for, as Ficino points out, the two words have the same derivation: 'All are called heroes, that is, lovers, from the Greek word "heros," which means "love".'[6] While some plays have heroes, such as Leontes in *The Winter's Tale*, who turn away from love only to regain it, his great tragic heroes are those who have advanced far on the path of love but, for some cause, are turned in their tracks and find themselves increasingly removed from their goal. At some point on this backward path, love is rejected: the love Ophelia offers Hamlet is rebuffed, Lear, so caught in self-esteem, fails to recognise the truth of Cordelia's love and Othello, with the murder of Desdemona, quenches the light of his love forever.

However, the relationship between Ficino and Shakespeare is more clearly explored if we follow some of the progressive paths of love taken by Shakespeare's young heroes. The first realisation of the lover that he has entered on the path of love comes literally like a bolt from the blue, when his heart is pierced by Cupid's dart. In *Love's Labour's Lost*, as the king succumbs to the beauty of the Princess, Berowne cries that he has been 'Shot, by heaven! Proceed sweet Cupid: thou hast thumped him with thy bird-bolt under the left pap.'[7] Now Cupid's arrow, as held in the bow of a plump cherub on a valentine card, has a far greater significance than is generally realised. For this 'bird-bolt' is none other than the ray of light that carries divine beauty straight from God to each of the worlds through which the lover will pass, and with which he will fall in love, on his return journey.

When first the hearts of Berowne and his friends have been pierced by Cupid's dart, their love for the beauty of their ladies lies in the world of appearances. Before they can become unified with their beloved through marriage in the world of the soul, they need to discover their own nature and to learn how to love the beauty of a virtuous life. In this, their mistresses become their teachers, and so, as the play ends, the Princess sends the King to spend a year in a remote hermitage learning the true nature of his love:

If this austere insociable life
Change not your offer made in heat of blood;
If frosts and fasts, hard lodging and thin weeds,
Nip not the gaudy blossoms of your love,
But that it bear this trial and last love;
Then at the expiration of a year,
Come challenge me, challenge me by these deserts,
And by this virgin palm now kissing thine,
I will be thine.[8]

At the same time, Rosaline sends Berowne to practise a virtuous life in a hospital where, instead of employing his sharp wit to mock and wound others, she asks him to use it for the finer purpose of bringing smiles to the faces of the sick, enforcing 'the pained impotent to smile.'[9]

After a false start, Romeo learns from his mistake and makes far greater progress along the path of love than Berowne. At the beginning of *Romeo and Juliet*, we find him in a state of unrequited love for Rosaline, heavy with misery and unwilling to dance with his friends. 'You are a lover,' Mercutio tells him, 'borrow Cupid's wings And soar with them above a common bound.'[10] But Romeo replies that he

is 'too sore empierced with his shaft To soar with his light feathers...
Under love's heavy burden do I sink.'[11] Romeo's problem is that his
love is misplaced; eager to enter on the path of love, he has chosen a
woman on whom, as Friar Lawrence has told him, he 'dotes' rather
than loves.[12] The world of appearances can delude and, in this situation,
Cupid's dart and wings encumber rather than aid love. Right judgement
is vital for the lover and, as soon as his eyes alight on Juliet, he realises
how mistaken his former love had been and that he 'ne'er saw true
beauty till this night.'[13] Now, truly pierced by the ray of beauty, he
recognises that the beauty of Juliet stems from the splendour of God
himself – 'For true love is nothing other than a certain effort of flying
up to divine beauty, aroused by the sight of corporeal beauty.'[14] Thus
their first encounter is in the form of a religious ritual: using the sonnet
form, Shakespeare presents Romeo as a pilgrim approaching a shrine
and the kiss that he requests from Juliet is received as a blessing.

Now no longer weighed down with the heaviness of a misplaced
love, Romeo soars with 'love's light wings'[15] over the orchard wall to
where Juliet stands on her balcony. In a letter explaining Plato's
description of the soul in *Phaedrus*, Ficino writes how mortal beings
'do not fly back to heaven, whence they fell by weight of their earthly
thoughts, until they begin to contemplate once more those divine natures
which they have forgotten.' Romeo is now at the point where, seeing
the reflection of divine beauty in his beloved, the lover will remember
that, before he became imprisoned in the body, he knew that beauty
face to face and, fired by this memory, the soul will shake its wings
and 'strive with all its might to reach the heavens.'[16]

The first impression that Romeo has of Juliet is the light she radiates:
'O, she doth teach the torches to burn bright!'[17] As Ficino tells us, this
light will lead him to truth: 'The beauty of bodies is a light; the beauty
of the soul is also a light. The light of the soul is truth'[18] and now,
when he next sees her on the balcony, he addresses her as the sun, the
physical representation of the light of God - for 'just as the sun gives
warmth and light to the body, so God offers the light of truth and the
warmth of love to souls.'[19] Before he leaves her garden he knows her
as his soul, 'It is my soul that calls upon my name'[20] and, in the

consummation of their marriage, he becomes unified with his soul. In a comedy, this would be the end of the play, but the lovers also represent the two sides of a divided society whose harmony has been disrupted. Separated by strife, it is not until their final reunion in death that peace can be restored.

By the opening of *The Merchant of Venice*, Bassanio is in no doubt that he has found his soul-mate and his heart has already been pierced, not only by the beauty of her person, but also by the virtues of her soul:

In Belmont is a lady richly left,
And she is fair, and (fairer than that word),
Of wondrous virtues...[21]

As Portia's suitor, he has to pass a trial of love which demands that, in order to win her as his wife, he must make a choice of three caskets. Faced with the lavish decoration of the gold and silver caskets, he is mindful that appearances are deceptive:

So may the outward shows be least themselves,
The world is still deceiv'd with ornament...[22]

Rightly choosing the leaden casket with the dull appearance, he finds, as Ficino says, that 'when the earthly grime has been removed you will at once see pure gold.'[23] For, hidden within, is indeed the pure gold, a portrait of Portia representing the greater beauty of the soul.

So Bassanio gains his soul but, before the union is consummated, he has a further test - of constancy. He leaves for Venice to attend the court of justice where Shylock is demanding his pound of flesh, given in bond by Antonio for the loan which enabled Bassanio to woo Portia. Before he goes, Portia gives him a ring which symbolises their union in love, freely giving herself and all she possesses. To give it away would be to give away his soul and, she tells him, 'presage the ruin of your love.'[24]

Now for Bassanio's soul to be so completely at one that it is ready for the next step into the angelic world of the mind, it must remain true and constant to itself. Constancy is standing firm in mind, to be steadfast and true; it is a quality of the higher mind, whose only movement, says Ficino, is that of turning itself towards God. The soul, on the other hand, may be moved unless it has the steadying influence of the mind. 'If there is any stability in the cognition of the soul, it is stable thanks to the mind rather than the soul.'[25] But without that steadying influence, Ficino continues, it may be swayed by sensation or reason – which is just what happens when Portia, disguised as the young doctor of law, asks for his ring as a reward. Overcome with the emotion of gratitude for saving the life of his friend, Bassanio is swayed by his reasonable argument and hands over the ring. Later, dressed in her true guise, Portia firmly rebukes him for his empty finger, symbol of his inconstancy:

> Even so void is your false heart of truth.
> By heaven I will ne'er come to your bed
> Until I see the ring![26]

Indeed, no union is possible if his soul is lost, but love is merciful, and Portia has the ring in her safe-keeping. Swearing his future constancy, she forgives him and together they return to Belmont for the consummation of their love.

Belmont, literally the 'hill of beauty,' represents the world of the soul, the place of beauty and harmony. Two lovers who have reached the world of the soul at Belmont and who are left there in charge while Portia performs her duty in the world, are Lorenzo and Jessica. The soul is the place of harmony where all come together, drawn by its beauty, in the concord of love. In the beauty of the starlit garden at Belmont, Lorenzo strives to hear the heavenly harmony sounded by the movement of the planets and the constellations of stars, which are the physical forms of the gods. As Berowne says in *Love's Labour's Lost*:

> ...when Love speaks, the voice of all the gods
> Make heaven drowsy with the harmony.[27]

In one of his letters, Ficino explains that, although we have known this harmony before we were born, now we are confined in our mortal bodies we can no longer hear this music of the spheres. That is, however, until love once more allows us to enter the world of the soul where, echoing the divine music formed in the mind of God, we may hear:

'...the motions and order of the heavens, by which the heavenly spheres and their orbits make a marvellous harmony. In both of these our soul took part before it was imprisoned in our bodies. But it uses the ears as messengers, as though they were chinks in this darkness. By the ears... the soul receives the echoes of that incomparable music, by which it is led back to the deep and silent memory of the harmony which it previously enjoyed.'[28]

Surely Shakespeare had Ficino's words in mind when he wrote Lorenzo's lines:

Here will we sit, and let the sounds of music
Creep in our ears – soft stillness and the night
Become the touches of sweet harmony:
Sit Jessica, – look how the floor of heaven
Is thick inlaid with patens of bright gold,
There's not the smallest orb which thou behold'st
But in his motion like an angel sings,
Still quiring to the young-ey'd cherubins;
Such harmony is in immortal souls,
But whilst this muddy vesture of decay
Doth grossly close it in we cannot hear it.[29]

The soul, Ficino continues, 'realises that as long as it is enclosed in the dark abode of the body it can in no way reach that music. It therefore strives wholeheartedly to imitate it.'[30] Thus, as the musicians enter, Lorenzo asks them to pierce Jessica's ears, 'her chinks in this darkness,' and 'draw her home' – that is, to the divine source of harmony:

With sweetest touches pierce your mistress ear,
And draw her home with music.[31]

Shakespeare's tragic heroes have knowledge of such heavenly harmony but have lost touch with love. Lear, in banishing his daughter,

Cordelia, is denying divine love within himself, so deep that she was unable to express it. During his long and painful journey back to redemption, in which he endures the anger of the gods brought to a climax in one tremendous storm, Cordelia becomes the custodian of his soul. Reunited with her towards the end of the play, he awakens to the sound of music, a sign that, as his soul has been restored, so has heavenly harmony. Indeed, we often find that, whenever a lover's lost soul is refound, music is being played. There is music as Pericles recognises his daughter, Marina, and when Leontes is reunited with his wife at the end of *A Winter's Tale*.

Ficino's letter continues by explaining how the lover, fired by the memory of the beauty he knew before he became imprisoned in his body, is overcome by a 'divine frenzy.' It was this madness, this burning desire for divine beauty, that drove Romeo over the orchard walls and it is the same frenzy that drives the poet to express that beauty. For, as Theseus says in *A Midsummer Night's Dream*:

The lunatic, the lover and the poet
Are of imagination all compact[32]

Poetic frenzy is inspired by the nine Muses, who incorporate all the powers of artistic expression that lie in the potential of the divine imagination: 'poetry springs from divine frenzy, frenzy from the Muses, and the Muses from Jove.'[33] All this takes place in the world of the angelic mind where, once he has reached this realm, man is enabled to create with the imagination of God, from which springs the whole creation. This world of the creative imagination is related by the Platonists to the element of fire, a divine fire that illuminates the mind and is the light of inspiration. It is this that Shakespeare is invoking in the words of his Chorus to *Henry V*:

O for a muse of fire that would ascend,
The brightest heaven of invention.[34]

Again, in one of his sonnets, Shakespeare addresses God who, within his own self, is the source of this fiery light and whom Ficino in this context calls Jove, as 'the tenth muse,' from whom the other nine spring and who gives light to the imagination:

For who's so dumb that cannot write to thee,
When thou thyself dost give invention light?
Be thou the tenth muse, ten times more in worth
Than those old nine which rhymers invocate...[35]

The divine fire is also the light of that same ray of beauty, Berowne's 'bird-bolt,' that first awakens man's love and, transcending 'the brightest heaven' of the angelic mind, returns to its source in itself, the one divine light of God. This is the moment that Shakespeare describes in *The Phoenix and the Turtle*, when the love of the turtle dove burns in 'mutual flame' with the fire of the phoenix and there is no distinction between them:

So between them love did shine
That the Turtle saw his right
Flaming in the Phoenix' sight
Either was the other's mine.[36]

Wishing to achieve this moment of blazing union, Ficino prays, 'O generous flame of our heart! Illumine us, we beg, shed your light on us and fire us, so that we inwardly blaze with the love of Your light...'[37]

Both fired by this light, Ficino and Shakespeare reached far beyond the corporeal body, 'this muddy vesture of decay,' to the divine beauty of 'the one truth, which is the single ray of the one God.'[38] As a philosopher, Shakespeare was inspired by the wisdom of Ficino; as a poet he was one who, as Ficino said, was 'inspired by the divine spirit' and gave 'forth with full voice the most solemn and glorious song.'

NOTES

1. Marsilio Ficino, *Commentary on Plato's Symposium on Love* (also referred to by Ficino as *De Amore*), trans. Sears Jayne, Texas, 1985, p.51-2. Hereafter referred to as *Comm.*
2. *Comm.* Intro. p.1
3. *Comm.* p.84
4. *Comm.* p.58

5. *Comm.* p.48
6. *Comm.* p.113
7. *Love's Labour's Lost* 4.3.21-2
   All quotations from Shakespeare are from the Arden editions.
8. *Love's Labour's Lost* 5.2.791-9
9. *Love's Labour's Lost* 5.2.846
10. *Romeo and Juliet* 1.4.17-8
11. *Romeo and Juliet* 1.4.19-22
12. *Romeo and Juliet* 2.3.78
13. *Romeo and Juliet* 1.5.51
14. *Comm.* p.172
15. *Romeo and Juliet* 2.2.66
16. *Letters* 1.7 pp.43-4 *The Letters of Marsilio Ficino*, 6 Vols., pub.
    Shepheard-Walwyn, London, 1975-99.
17. *Romeo and Juliet* 1.5.44
18. *Comm.* p.142
19. *Comm.* p.46
20. *Romeo and Juliet* 2.2.164
21. *The Merchant of Venice* 1.2.161-3
22. *The Merchant of Venice* 3.2.73-4
23. *Letters* 1.110 p.164
24. *The Merchant of Venice* 3.2.173
25. *Comm.* p.48
26. *The Merchant of Venice* 5.1.189-191
27. *Love's Labour's Lost* 4.3.340-1
28. *Letters* 1.7 p.45
29. *The Merchant of Venice* 5.1.55-65
30. *Letters* 1.7 p.45-6
31. *The Merchant of Venice* 5.1.66-68
32. *A Midsummer Night's Dream* 5.1.7-8
33. *Letters* 1.7 p.46
34. *Henry V* Prologue 1-2
35. *Sonnet* 38.7-10
36. *The Phoenix and the Turtle* 33-36
37. *Letters* 1.123 pp.190-1
38. *Letters* 1.42 p.84

Music and Marsilio Ficino

JOHN STEWART ALLITT

The man who has no music in himself,
Nor is not mov'd with concord of sweet sounds
Is fit for treasons, stratagems, and spoils;
The motions of his spirit are dull as night,
And his affections dark as Erebus:
Let no such man be trusted. *

SHAKESPEARE'S words are set within the tradition received from the Florentine Academy of which Marsilio Ficino (1433-99) was the leading thinker. His translations of Plato, together with various Neoplatonic and Hermetic texts, laid the foundation of the new wave of classical thought in the West. The ransacking and betrayal by the West which had led to the collapse of the Byzantine Empire at the hands of the Moors is a scandalous episode in the chapters of history. For centuries the West had erred from Orthodoxy and by its greed and machiavellian lust for power had laid the foundations enabling modern secularism gradually to mature. It is ironic that the Medici, who ideally fitted into this role of the avaricious 'new' world order, and who through the Councils of Ferrara and Florence (1438-45), had gained a fascination for the East, became Ficino's patrons. Consider, for example, Benozzo Gozzoli's frescoes in the Medici Chapel where the Emperor John Palaeologus VIII, Joseph, Patriarch of Constantinople and Lorenzo de'Medici are depicted as representing the Magi coming to worship the incarnate Lord. There are few better indications in art of the change of consciousness taking place within the West from personhood to individualism, from ikon to figurative representation.

* *The Merchant of Venice,* Vi 83-88

Besides the Filioque Clause and other doctrinal points, such as the Augustinian view of sin, the gulf separating the West from Orthodoxy was becoming clearer by Ficino's century. The East over the centuries had grown naturally with the legacy of classical learning. Church fathers such as Dionysius the Areopagite, Gregory of Nyssa and Maximus the Confessor had all led on where the old learning had waned, without a break. Indeed, in the narthexes of Greek churches it is possible to find Plato, Aristotle and other classical philosophers and writers portrayed on the ceilings as forerunners to the Incarnation. The West under the guidance of the papacy had set out on another course, that of a rival empire and proud empirical thought.

When the texts of the ancient philosophers during the fifteenth century became more widely available through Ficino's editions and translations, the Western response consequently lacked the natural growth of the East. A separation of ascetic and speculative thought became immediately recognizable; for example, Savonarola and his denunciation of the Medici. Furthermore the Aristotelian roots of Thomism, sanctioned by the papacy at the expense of the Platonic tradition, helped to lead on to the new science and the eventual birth of modernism.

Therefore, when considered in the light of Orthodoxy, Ficino, regardless of his many noble sentiments and insights, appears as an uneasy, late attempt to graft on to the tree of tradition certain 'new-found' truths and enlightenments. The East, fortunately saved through its monasticism, did not bury its head in the sand and took a measured interest in the developments taking place in Florence. For example, it is possible to find Ficino's texts in monastic libraries on the peninsula of Mount Athos. The response to these writings must have been mixed. Perhaps there was perceived in them a mingling of the good and the misguided due to an individual struggling to interpret a 'lost' tradition which had never ceased being nourished in the East.

When the Renaissance is considered by the public at large it is generally the visual arts which come to mind, then possibly its literature, music being often unfortunately overlooked. However, during these years the speculative foundations of the science of western 'classical' music were laid. Generally the influence of the Florentine Academy with its orientation towards Platonism and the Hermetic tradition is considered by many to have come to an end in Italy with Pico della Mirandola: this is due to the gathering force of Inquisition and Counter-Reformation. This is not strictly correct, for the ancient wisdom lived on among theorists and in particular through the growth of academies and music schools. From these developed, as said above, what we now term 'classical' music – a flow of maturing expression developing until the signs of disintegration began to surface, especially in the nineteenth century under the influence of Berlioz and Wagner. For example, if we are to study Palestrina or Byrd, Corelli or Tartini, the Bach Family or Handel, Haydn or Mozart, Paisiello or Donizetti, then it is back to the classical science and practice of music we have to refer, that is, if we are seeking to understand their intellectual and creative worlds.

The development and emergence of Western classical music owes a lion's share to Ficino. Franchino Gaffurio, Gioseffo Zarlino and the Florentine Academy of the Bardi circle drew heavily on the stimulus of Ficino and turned to study afresh the ancient philosophy from Pythagoras to Boethius. If we have an art form today called 'opera', its roots have to be traced back to the Renaissance and the rediscovery in the West of ancient texts thanks to Ficino's editions, translations and commentaries. Originally, 'opera' was not associated with jet-set singers and conductors, but the 'work', the great work of understanding the relationship between the cosmos and humanity, the passions and their consequences on fate and destiny, the root cause of the destructive anger of tragedy, the laughter and the antics of comedy's social observations (*ridendo castigat mores*), and the escape into the ideal love found in the pastoral tradition. For opera, the 'work', the profundity of myth and the example of classical history became of paramount importance. It is enough to recall the influence of the Orphic tale over Poliziano, Peri and his poet Rinuccini, Monteverdi, and across the years to Bertoni and Gluck. Likewise the fame of Metastasio's libretti held up numerous heroic examples taken from Greek and Roman history. The poet's influence may be felt right up to Mayr's *Demetrio* (1823).

Even Felice Romani, the most sought after Italian librettist of the first half of the nineteenth century, was to turn his back on romanticism in favour of the classical ideal.

It is a fascinating tale which has been for the greater part overlooked in favour of the frivolities of singers, the tragedies of composers' lives and bland musical analysis.

Ficino's essential contribution was to insist on the correspondence between the macrocosm and the microcosm, ensuring that the Muses and music were intimately related, and linking the planets to the human passions. He asked, for example, the fundamental question, why had Plato considered the soul as a musical consonance:

> Musical consonance occurs in the element [Air] which is the mean of all, and reaches the ears through motion, spherical motion: so that it is not surprising that it should be fitting to the soul, which is both the mean of things, and the origin of circular motion. In addition, music, more than anything else perceived by the senses, conveys, as if animated, the emotions and thoughts of the singer's or player's soul to the listener's soul; thus it preeminently corresponds with the soul. Moreover, as regards sight, although visual impressions are in a way pure, yet they lack the effectiveness of motion, and are usually perceived only as an image, without reality; normally, therefore, they move the soul only slightly. Smell, taste, and touch are entirely material, and rather titillate the sense organs than penetrate the depths of the soul. But musical sound by the movement of the air moves the body; by purifying air it excites the aerial spirit which is the bond of body and soul; by emotion it affects the senses and at the same time the soul; by meaning it works on the mind; finally, by the very movement of the subtle air it penetrates strongly; by its contemperation it flows smoothly; by the conformity of its quality it floods us with a wonderful pleasure: by its nature, both spiritual and material, it at once seizes, and claims as its own, man in his entirety.[1]

Ficino's insistence on the role of the element of air goes back to many sources, for example the alchemical tradition and writers such as Petrarch. Air is perceived as the element which modelled the macrocosm and which in man inspired his imagination and intellect. Thus air is the supreme element for communication and life. The aerial spirit is the bond between the soul and the body: it discovers an echo with the *spiritus*, the subtle substance permeating the body, activating the life-force and psychic life within us all.[2] To breathe correctly, as a musician or singer must do, is to inhale more than just 'air', for correct breathing is essential to the intellectual and creative life of a person. Intellectuals, Ficino noted, are prone to exhaust their *spiritus* due to their sedentary way of life. No wonder Ficino spoke of taking life-giving walks amidst verdant nature!

Music, as in Dante's *Paradiso*, is the quality of the higher order of things.[3] The harmony of sounds is the secret of our soul's health. When in health, the soul and Apollo's heavenly lyre vibrate to the same ratios. When sick, the soul lacks vibrant harmony and becomes 'out of tune'. All harmony is expressed through correct proportion and relationship:

> Our soul contains all the same proportions as the soul of the world (*anima mundi*). None of these ratios is mathematical: rather, they have a natural force. They are not to be thought of as solely mathematical ratios but as machinating and generating.[4]

A mistake often made by students of Alberti and Palladio has been to understand simply the mathematical at the expense of the 'breathing', imaginative quality of proportion. Number in this context is as the literal is to the allegorical, moral and anagogical levels of insight. As we know, Michelangelo reacted strongly to Alberti's concept of architecture being 'frozen music', for, he said, we can move and breathe within and without a building. If so, how can it be 'frozen'? Furthermore the monochord was an intrument used for contemplation and insight, not mere measurement.

Ficino understood that song is the most evocative and 'most powerful imitator of all things', for it 'imitates the intentions and the passions of the soul as well as words.' Song may imitate, better evoke, the celestial worlds, and when it so does 'it wonderfully arouses our spirit upwards to the celestial influence and the celestial influence down to our spirit.'

This imaginative world of Ficino is admirably caught in a poem by Giovanni Marenzi, fortunately saved through being copied out by Donizetti's teacher, Simon Mayr, in his teaching notebooks. The following quotations will give the reader the feel of a poem which admirably captures the Platonic world of the Italian academies inspired through Ficino's work:[5]

> O Soul (*anima mundi*) who animates these earthly shapes,
> bestow their form, rejoice in harmony –
> who are indeed yourself, true harmony
> behold your contours, known to you alone
> radiant though as yet you dwell in sleep,
> oppressed, imprisoned by the miry clay;
> if with frail tongue you can utter your first origin,
> speak out, that I may declare on paper
> the value, order, out of music's modes.

> Since I compose
> reveal your inspiration,
> your rich inebriation.
> Should my song fail
> to free you from your dungeon,
> yet shall you still return
> to beauty,
> your first habitation,
> where each true melody is freely born,
> compared to which
> our earth is but a shadow.

> If truth was uttered by Pythagoras
> in the sovereign intellect, Number was the prime idea,
> when He fused his first Idea with ice,
> thus tempering his heat,
> Number was foremost in his thought.
> Desirous to form man content and just,

He grounded him in Number,
from which He had created this great mass,
of stars, moon, sun –
Number was to be his first example
granting the Spirit wings to rise to the divine temple.

Since thus the soul is touched by Number's concord
as a well-tempered harp
utters divine and ardent ecstasy,
what were the soul to hear
the various sounds concert among themselves,
as spheres, now slow, now fast, which travel the heavens?...

Gaffurio, drawing on Ficino, associated the modes with the planets and Muses. This was soon to inspire composers to note the difference in quality between the major and the minor and the various keys into which the scale (*scala* = ladder) may be locked and unlocked. The passions became in time associated with the different keys and consequently the art of harmony became the great secret for penetrating, arousing and healing the passions. The science of music was understood to relate to the order of things. This influence, begun with the theorists of the Renaissance, may be found as late as our own century in the writings of composers such as Respighi. The following interesting quotations from classical sources in the next paragraph come from his book *Orpheus*, which he wrote with Sebastiano Luciano in 1925:

'*Musica nihil aliud est quam omnium ordinem scire*'(Hermes Trismegistus). 'Music is the healer of the passions – *Musicam docet Amor*' (Plato). The right use of melody and rhythm became the main aim of the Italian composers. 'Some philosophers in the past termed rhythm as masculine and melody as feminine. It is a fact that melody is nothing without form... rhythm gives it form and suggests an ordered movement (Aristides Quintilianus). Melody became the hallmark of the Italians and it could be said that they intuitively understood that 'melody is a succession of sounds that call to one another' (St John Damascene). It is the manner in which the sounds call to one another that a melody may evoke melancholia, love, anger, sadness, and so forth. In this context opera was to be Italy's great contribution to the West and its music. This said, the nation's development of the string family away from the ancient consort of viols and the consequent development of the art of the concerto formed the basis to late eighteenth and nineteenth century Western music.'

Fundamental for Ficino was the realization that our health and the music we entertain are intimately linked. He makes this abundantly clear in a letter.[6] Bearing in mind Ficino's insight and Shakespeare's advice quoted at the beginning of this short contribution, one should take great care in handing over the health of one's body to a medical practitioner. The horrors to which many are subjected today at the hands of doctors and surgeons would have been foreseen by the wise of old. To separate music and consequently the *gnosis* upon which music is based from medicine would have been considered tantamount to folly, for it negates the relationship of our passions, our psychic life, to our body. Ficino's advice is to seek out true music, as opposed to noise, and then never to abandon it. It is one of the secrets for dying with grace.

NOTES

1. Marsilio Ficino *Commentaria in Timaeum* S29 - his *Opera Omnia* (Basel 1576) 1453, quoted by DP Walker *Spiritual and Demonic Magic from Ficino to Campanella* (London 1958) 8-9.

2. Ficino, through his idealism, overlooks the 'warfare' of the angelic hosts and the 'fierce Prince of the air', Lucifer. The use of sound may produce diabolical energies as well as energies for the good. A composer, in the modern sense of the word, may influence for harm as well as for healing. It is a matter of discerning the spirits. A composer will draw on the energies of his particular level of consciousness.

3. There is no music in the *Inferno*, just cacophony. Music, except as an expression of worship and prayer, is not encouraged in the *Purgatorio*, for there is too much inner work to be done there!

4. *Constat enim anima nostra ex omnibus proportionibus quibus anima mundi. Qua quidem sicut nec in illa, ita nec in nostra rationes quaedam mathematicae sunt, sed potius naturales uim habentes, ad proportiones mathematicas non iudicandas solum,*

sed machinandas etiam atque generandas. Ficino *Commentaria* (Turin 1959) quoted from Claude V Palisca *Humanism in Italian Renaissance musical thought* (New Haven and London 1985) 170.

5. See John Stewart Allitt *J S Mayr – Father of 19th century Italian music* (Shaftesbury 1989) 124-27(author's translation).

6. *The Letters of Marsilio Ficino*, trans. vol 1 (London 1975) 141-144 (letter 92).

Ficino on Law and Justice

L L BLAKE

*Affairs of state cannot be properly and successfully
conducted without divine help**

THE TRANSLATORS of the recent series of books entitled *The Letters of
Marsilio Ficino* say in their preface that Ficino 'related all activities
to the central aim of Man: to return to his divine source'.[1] He wrote to
men in many different professions; and certainly those letters directed
to lawyers are meant to remind them of the divinity which informs and
graces their vocation. In his eyes, 'high also is the office of lawyer
among men. He is the defender of the citizens as a whole, the general
oracle of the state, and the interpreter of the divine mind and will'.[2]

Writing in such terms may well have been intended to elevate the
recipients' own views of their profession. Praise, rather than criticism,
was the method employed by Ficino to illuminate the virtues which
might be practised by individual men, thus leading them back to their
divine origin. In a letter entitled by Ficino himself in his collection,
Legitimi iurisconsulti partes (the role of the true man of law), addressed
to Pier Filippo Perugini, whom Ficino calls 'the illustrious man of
law', the following passage appears:

> What, therefore, is more beautiful on earth than an impartial
> interpreter of justice and law? What, on the other hand, more
> shameful than a biased interpreter?
>
> I see that you want to consider the cast and nature of the
> true man of law. What a beautiful and wonderful spectacle! His
> soul is the worship of God; his spirit is the care of his country's

* Ficino, *Letters*, Vol 5, p.50

law; his brain, clear-sighted judgment; his eyes and tongue, doctrine; his breast, strong memory; his heart, right will; his hands, the performance of right will; and his feet, perseverance; the whole, justice and dignity.³

Setting aside the propensity of the times, and of Ficino, to indulge in a certain grandiloquence of style, the letter nevertheless appears to answer a question raised by Perugino as to what, exactly, his profession should mean to him. This is not often the case among lawyers today, who, if they consider it at all, are satisfied with the rewards of the job and the envy caused to their clients. Not many pause to ask themselves how they might serve their fellow-men and, at the same time, work towards the liberation of the soul. Yet, if they do pause, Ficino offers them one of the finest insights into the nature of a lawyer's true being that exists in Renaissance literature.

Ficino wrote about 'the goodness and dignity of a lawyer' in a letter to Angelo Niccolini:⁴

A painter who makes corrupt use of his art is not necessarily a bad painter because of this, but he is a bad man. Thus a good painter is not the same as a good man. This is evident, for there is a great deal of difference between goodness and painting. And the same applies to the rest of the arts. But a lawyer who makes unlawful use of the law, is both a bad lawyer and a bad man; while the upright lawyer is also an upright man and citizen. The relationship between the profession of civil law and the virtue of man is as close as this.

He who defaces a coin, a thing of very little value, dug from the bowels of the earth, is punished by human law, as you know, with the severest penalty. Thus how sternly is the man punished by divine law who corrupts the most precious law itself, which has been sent to us from heaven!

'The relationship between the profession of civil law and the virtue of man is as close as this'. Indeed it is. We, in Great Britain, are fortunate in having judges and lawyers who are not corrupt; but consider the loss of trust and human dignity in countries where the law governing men's lives is abused. Where then is the confidence to build a secure and healthy society?

Ficino repeats the admonition concerning the corruption of the sacred law in a letter, *De officiis*, to the learned Cherubino Quarquagli:[5]

> ...[the duty] of the lawyer [is] to be the most venerable of men, and to know that a man who corrupts the sacred law should be punished as for a sacrilege by a more severe penalty than a man who debases the coinage.

He ends the letter: 'Since man cannot live content in earth, he should realise that he is indeed a citizen of heaven, but an inhabitant in earth. He should therefore strive to think, say and do nothing which does not become a citizen of the kingdom of heaven'.

The importance to the state of good lawyers is recognised in a letter entitled *Lex et iustitia*:[6]

> You persuaded me to render the *Laws* of Plato from Greek into Latin and the great Cosimo also encouraged me to do the same work. This I have already done, and all the more willingly because I considered the state to need the best lawyers more than good merchants or doctors. In the same degree as Minos benefited the Greeks more than Galen did, so is the soul superior to the body or the spirit, and eternal life to the temporal. Indeed, commerce appears to be the body of the state, medicine the spirit, and law the soul.

'The remarkable qualities of Ficino's letters are the more apparent when one considers the times in which they were written', say the translators in discussing the Pazzi conspiracy of 1477-8.[7] 'It is as if the most violent and lawless times call forth the most sublime statements of philosophy, and make them peculiarly appropriate.' The times were heady with conflicting views of the law and of mastership in the state. The Roman law of Justinian was creeping into European jurisdictions, with its emphasis on 'What pleases the prince has the force of law',[8] which gave rise to absolute monarchies and to the powerful doctrines of Machiavelli.

In England, at about the same time, Sir John Fortescue was asserting the English law of freedom:[9]

For the king of England is not able to change the laws of his kingdom at pleasure, for he rules his people with a government not only regal but also political. If he were to preside over them with a power entirely regal, he would be able to change the laws of his realm, and also impose on them tallages and other burdens without consulting them; this is the sort of dominion which the civil laws indicate when they state that *What pleased the prince has the force of law*. But the case is far otherwise with the king ruling his people politically, because he is not able himself to change the laws without the assent of his subjects nor to burden an unwilling people with strange imposts, so that, ruled by laws that they themselves desire, they freely enjoy their properties and are despoiled neither by their own king nor any other.

So much is this the natural language of freedom for the English that, today, at the millennium, they find themselves in a dilemma as to how far to advance along the road to European sovereignty. Assuredly they will have to come to a decision, whether to adopt the maxim of Justinian as the guiding principle of their law, or to abide by the keynote set for them by Bracton in the thirteenth century, *The king must not be under man but under God and the law, because law makes the king.*[10]

Ficino would have had no difficulty accepting the last statement:[11]

Furthermore, when he is appointed an officer of government, he will have the law always in view as if it were God. He will not, indeed, consider himself a master of the law, but its faithful interpreter and devoted servant.

And, in the same letter, he put divine law first, natural law second:

That divine law by which the universe abides and is governed, kindles in our minds at their creation the inextinguishable light of natural law, by which good and evil are tested. From this natural law, which is a spark of the divine, the written law arises like a ray from that spark. Moreover, these three laws, divine, natural and written, teach each man what justice is, so that there is scarcely any room left for sinners to plead complete ignorance as an excuse for their faults.

As to natural law, Ficino says:[12]

The Mosaic precepts are distinguished in the works of the theologians as being of two kinds. Some pertain to natural and moral law, others to rites and the administration of justice. The first were given by God to Moses and the people; the second Moses himself ordained when divinely inspired. Again, the first are given to the whole human race to be kept for all time. The second bind the Jews alone; that is, until the coming of the Messiah himself. The first precepts which we have mentioned are so universal that they could be known to anyone, even of little education, simply through natural understanding. For what else is contained in them other than worship of the one God and the leading of a lawful life.

There is evidence in the letters that Ficino also had in mind a kind of law equivalent to our Common Law. This is based on custom and reason and is largely applied throughout the English-speaking world. St German had described the Common Law as based 'upon divers general customs of old time used through all the realm, which have been accepted and approved by our sovereign lord the king, and his progenitors, and all his subjects. And because the said customs be neither against the law of God, nor the law of reason, and have been alway taken to be good and necessary for the commonwealth of all the realm; therefore they have obtained the strength of a law...'[13]

In Letter 1 of Volume 4 of *The Letters*, Ficino says that one of the ways in which human laws are accepted or kept in being is 'through arguments from common custom based on human and natural principles'.

Elsewhere[14] he writes:

...yet there is but one public law. This is the common rule of living justly, which leads to the public happiness. God and nature prepare us for this law, regulations guide us towards it, and God alone finally makes us conform to it.

This extract is from a letter headed *Lex et iustitia*. Ficino was as concerned with justice as he was with law. From his Platonic reading he would have known that the two ran together, as in *The Laws*,[15] where law is the straight line and justice the punisher:

'Friends', we say to them, — 'God, as the old tradition declares, holding in his hand the beginning, middle, and end of all that is, moves according to his nature in a straight line towards the accomplishment of his end. Justice always follows him, and is the punisher of those who fall short of the divine law...'

On this scale Ficino is right to speak about justice in terms of administration; justice cannot alter the law, but it is how the law is administered. His master, Plato, again:[16]

When anger and fear, and pleasure and pain, and jealousies and desires, tyrannise over the soul, whether they do any harm or not, — I call all this injustice. But when the opinion of the best, in whatever part of human nature states or individuals may suppose that to dwell, has dominion in the soul and orders the life of every man, even if it be sometimes mistaken, yet what is done in accordance therewith, and the principle in individuals which obeys this rule, and is best for the whole life of man, is to be called just...

It is plain that Ficino was a just man. This is the aspect of him which, it is hoped, this short essay will convey. He put God first in all his deliberations; but if the modern reader finds God unacceptable, then Ficino would urge him to direct his efforts towards truth and goodness:[17]

Therefore, so that we can trust something, let us now trust truth itself which, since it admits no ignorance or deception, certainly keeps no one in ignorance and deceives nobody. Furthermore, so that we can place our hope in something somewhere that is good, let us place our hope in the good itself which, since it does no evil and suffers no injustice, never disappoints those who hope for it and never abandons those who love it. It has given them light that they may hope and set them afire that they may love; for the movement towards the good can depend on no other source than the good itself and can return there by no other means than that by which it came forth.

NOTES

1. *The Letters of Marsilio Ficino*, translated by the School of Economic Science, London, (Shepheard-Walwyn), Vol 1, p 20
2. *The Letters*, Vol 1, p 121
3. *The Letters*, Vol 1, pp 150-151
4. *The Letters*, Vol 1, pp 120-121
5. *The Letters*, Vol 2, p 66
6. *The Letters*, Vol 1, pp 40-41
7. *The Letters*, Vol 4, p 73 *et seq*
8. *Institutes* 1.2
9. *In Praise of the Laws of England*, Chrimes ed., (CUP 1942), p 25
10. *On the Laws and Customs of England*, Woodbine, ed. (Harvard 1968) Vol II, p33
11. *The Letters*, Vol 1, pp 146-147
12. *The Letters*, Vol 4, p 64
13. *Doctor and Student, c.* 1532, chap 7
14. *The Letters*, Vol 1, p 41
15. Jowett, 716
16. Jowett, *The Laws*, 864 V
17. *The Letters*, Vol 4, p 4

Translating Ficino

PATRICIA GILLIES

If each of us, essentially, is that which is greatest within us, which always remains the same and by which we understand ourselves, then certainly the soul is the man himself and the body but his shadow. *

THIS was the first letter our particular translation group was given to translate thirty years ago. As members of the School of Economic Science, which studies Economics and Philosophy, some of us became interested in the writings of Marsilio Ficino, the Renaissance humanist and philosopher. No full English translation existed of his volumes of letters, and so we undertook the work. The group consisted of three or four people and apart from one lady who had a Double First in Classics our Latin was rusty. Our intention was to translate the letter above at home, and return the next week when a final version would be hammered out in the group.

The work at home was laboured, the 16th century Basle text was unfamiliar, the sentences were littered with pronouns which did not seem to relate to anything in particular and there was no insight into the Latin construction, let alone the subtleties of philosophical thought. When the translation was presented to the group a week later the lack of practice and comprehension was all too obvious. Over the following weeks the work was slow, people were reluctant to surrender a well-turned phrase or a specific understanding of the text or anxious not to make a mistake and appear an idiot. There were one or two who dominated either through greater skill in Latin or English or force of personality. If a passage was particularly difficult I arrogantly believed

* Ficino, *Letters*, Vol 1, letter 15

Ficino had got his grammar wrong until the same construction by Cicero was discovered in Kennedy's *Latin Primer* or the Lewis & Short *Dictionary*.

In spite of these difficulties the quality of translation skill improved. This came about in several ways:

In the 1970's it was suggested in our school of philosophy that to lead a happy and philosophical life, a degree of measure would help. This meant that in a day one hour should be set aside for meditation, three hours for gentle restful study and nine hours for our chosen work in life. In my case, one to one and a half hours a day was devoted to translating Ficino, the work was so interesting that this took place whatever the circumstances, even while moving house.

Every summer the Renaissance Group, which consisted of three or four small translation groups, went away for a week of translating. We got up early, meditated, and then began translating. We had four one-and-a-half hour study periods a day. These were punctuated by time for self catering and physical activity like gardening or walking and each evening we would all meet together to discuss our findings and then have dinner accompanied by magnificent wines. All fourteen or fifteen of us, as well as becoming far more proficient in Latin, also developed specific talents: a greater knowledge of Ficino's correspondents, a greater understanding of the politics and history of the time, a comprehensive knowledge of the Latin texts, manuscript or printed editions, a knowledge of Ficino's source material, Plato, Virgil, the Bible. But these activities never really had the same fascination as the process of translation itself. One week I had to translate all day, every day while the texts were being annotated. Naturally, the skill improved, although it is always easier to translate in a group than on one's own at home. During these weeks we often accomplished more than in a year of weekly meetings.

Here is an attempt to describe the process of translating. Those with a quick and nimble Latin wit please forgive:

Conatus sum diebus superioribus ideam philosophi Platonicis coloribus pingere.   Letter 19 Vol 3 Life of Plato.

First of all it is important to read the Latin to oneself in the mind, really listening to the sound of it. One sentence at a time. If the mechanical part of mind starts working words out straight away the skill in translating will develop much more slowly and the possibility of hearing Ficino actually speaking will be lost. Next, skill is needed to begin working it out.

A good dictionary and a Latin grammatical primer are essential.

Conatus sum from *Conor:*	I undertake, endeavour, attempt. *Conor* takes an infinitive.
Pingere:	To represent pictorially.
Ideam:	Accusative singular depending on *pingere*. Idea.
Philosophi:	Genitive singular, of a philosopher.
Platonicis coloribus:	In Platonic colours.
Diebus superioribus:	Ablative plural, time within which, In the preceding days.

This could be explained in far greater detail, but the point is that every word has to be carefully accounted for, precision and attention are needed not to gloss over a word thinking 'I know this already'. It is just at this point that a translation goes wrong and because 'I know this' has been thought, it is difficult to see where the mistake has been made, this little formulation throws up a smoke screen.

Next the magical part, hard to describe. Suddenly, the understanding presents itself, not in English, but just the understanding. The English follows on, though the translation may not yet be elegant or fluent, this is where a group would help to refine it. A final version of this sentence would be:

In the last few days I have tried to paint the ideal form of a philosopher in Platonic colours.

The word *ideam* has been translated as Ideal Form, based on Plato's Ideas, archetypes, perfection, not subject to decay.

The translation of this letter continues:

However if I had brought Plato himself into our midst, I would assuredly not have pointed to some picture of the ideal form of a true philosopher, but to the ideal form itself. Therefore let us look closely at our Plato, so that we may see equally philosopher, philosophy and the ideal form itself, at one and the same time.

A different process takes over: How can philosopher, philosophy and the ideal form be present at the same time? What does Ficino mean, he is probably speaking from knowledge but is this in my experience? Sometimes the mind gives up at this point and sits still in silent contemplation. Sometimes, though very rarely, one is transported to the world of the Platonic Academy, where the Masters sit in the company of the Good, compassionately overviewing the world of men as they learn to play out the game of life. Sometimes, one may even see Plato himself entering a room entirely present, free from past or future, entirely good, entirely beautiful. A formless form. But, although one may experience occasional glimpses of a higher order, the work of translating nowadays takes place in the groups. The day to day work on grammar is still practised as homework with exercises from various grammar books and, if a letter is particularly complicated, the text is reflected on at times between our weekly meetings.

Here then is a brief description of the work of a translation group. The first part describes the grammar practice, the second part gives some details needed to understand the letter itself which we were translating and the last part is in the form of a dialogue between the three members of the translation group: P.G., P.O. and E.W.

Each evening begins and ends with a moment of silence. We begin with grammar, a fifteen minute look at Colebourne's grammar book, in order to reacquaint or introduce ourselves to various aspects of the language. We have all completed 27A, an exercise on Final Relative Clauses from English into Latin. There is a discussion on sentence 1: 'I have been sent here to work with you.' Bill, who is taking the grammar session, is unfamiliar with the translation of 'here'. It has been translated *huc:* 'hither', not *hic:* 'here'. The Latin is more precise than the English where the distinction between the words, 'here', 'hither' and 'hence' have fallen out of use. Everyone reads out a sentence in English then gives their translation, *ex tempore*, if they did not do the exercises, or from their homework. Some have spent time to produce an elegant Latin translation, others are more simple and straightforward. Charlotte, mother of four, has completed hers in the car on the way to the group. The grammar session completed we split into two groups. One group is a revision group the other, ours, is translating.

Throughout the years we have worked with manuscripts and printed editions of the Books of Ficino's letters to arrive at a definitive text for translation. At the moment, Book 8, we are using two texts, one is an edition printed in Basle (1576), related to the Venice printed edition of 1495, mentioned by Ficino himself, and the other a manuscript, L28, now held in the Laurenziana library in Florence, copied in 1490.

To begin with we read Letter 830 right through in the Latin from the Basle edition and then briefly return to the title. *Honesta exactio ab amico*. We are not sure how *exactio* should be translated, it could be 'An honest demand from a friend' but we decide to wait to the end before finalising it.

After the title, each letter is addressed to somebody: sometimes Ficino addresses Mankind; this time it is:

Marsilio Ficino to Pico della Mirandola: greetings.

Pico, 1463-1494: A brilliant scholar who published in 1486 a polemic thesis *On all knowledge* which became known as *The 900 Conclusions*. A Papal commission declared thirteen theses to be heretical or suspect and Pico fled to Paris, where he was imprisoned. Through the intercession of Lorenzo de' Medici and King Charles VIII of France, he was pardoned and allowed to settle in Florence. He studied Hebrew, Chaldaeic and Arabic and was the first Western scholar to acquire a knowledge of the Jewish Cabbala which he tried to harmonise with Christian theology. He died aged 31.

This is useful information taken from the Notes on Ficino's Correspondents in Volume 3, as it will help us to understand the letter as it unfolds. We are also told in previous letters, which we did not translate, that Pico had a habit of not returning books, priceless possessions in 1486. Further information on the people mentioned in the letter will be explained as the translation of the letter proceeds.

We compare the Basle edition with L28. To our surprise we discover that L28 has a further nine lines, an unusual occurrence and we wonder why these were deleted from the Basle edition. Was there anything in the letter that Ficino would not have wanted to be published? L28 tells us that the letter was written in September 1486, Pico goes to Rome in March 1487 with his completed work, so he would still be in the middle of preparing his thesis.

Here is a dialogue between the three translators in a group working on this letter. Ficino's words are of course our translation, not as yet finalised as it has to go to the Revision Group, who will make sure that there have been no obvious mistakes, they will also polish it.

The translation, one sentence at a time, is undertaken by one person, the others helping if need be. The words are looked up and the grammar is considered, we finally arrive at:

Ficino: *I had no wish to trouble you to send us Mohamed while some were pressing you for other authors. (aliorum)*

P.G.: Ficino often speaks about books as if they were living entities. Do you remember in letter 815 he speaks of Plato leaving Italy to go to Francesco Bandini in Hungary?

E.W.: Yes, here he is speaking about Mohamed as if he is a living being, not a book.

P.O.: But we cannot translate *aliorum* as 'other authors', Ficino is actually talking about borrowed books not people.

P.G.: Shall we change 'authors' to 'writers' then?

Silence; for lack of anything better this is accepted.

The letter continues, as usual we read the Latin and then translate:

Ficino: *If he (Mohammed) were to grow much older away from his native land, I am afraid he would eventually be incapable of returning and, since you are a man of compassion, please see to it that he comes back in good time.*

This passage is difficult to translate until Basle is compared with L28. Basle has *ante* (before) instead of *autem* (moreover), *si* (if) instead of *sit* (is) and *humilitate* (humility) instead of *humanitate* (humanity, compassion). So, since *ante, si* and *humilitate* do not make sense in the context, L28 must be the more accurate version.

Ficino: *But if you are to keep him (Mohamed) with you as your guest a few days more, at least send Avicenna straight away, who is discoursing on the Divine Promise just after Mohamed. For this dissertation is all-important to me, particularly now. You will find it at the end of the Koran or a little further on.*

Avicenna is a 9th century astrologer and Plotinus wrote on astrology. In 1486 Ficino would need Avicenna to clarify his commentaries to Plotinus which he was working on at the time. We are unsure what the Divine Promise would be, or what 'a little further on' refers to, we will seek help on this, but we translate the passage as accurately as possible. This then is all there is to the Basle, there now remains the further nine lines in L28, the manuscript.

It is not easy to read and the translation is laboured. We look up some of the words in the dictionary and consider the grammar.

P.G.:   I suppose a rough translation of this passage would be: 'About Plotinus, I am not going to send either the commentary or the printed edition until I hear this work of yours has come *excidisse* to you from the heart; then it will seem that it is Plotinus who is with you.'

P.O.:   Er no, I don't think this is accurate, I would say: 'Until I see that this fortune has fallen out *excidisse* to you from your breast.'

P.G.:   It says in Lewis and Short that this is a very rare use of *excidisse*, your translation does not make any sense. Anyway, heart is a much better translation than breast.

Knowledge is supposed to arise from the heart, one wouldn't say knowledge comes from the breast or the chest or the pectoris.

P.O.:   But your translation is far-fetched, it is guessing at the meaning. What do you think Eileen?

P.G.:   It's not guessing. If knowledge arises from the heart, then the knowledge of Plotinus would arise from Pico's own heart, not from Ficino's translation or commentary. Ficino is actually instructing Pico, he is telling him not to be cerebral.

P.O.:   I'm not at all sure you're right. Let's go on to the next sentence, perhaps that will clarify this.

P.G.:   No, each sentence is complete in itself. This wouldn't help, we ought at least to get out a translation of this before we move on.

P.O.& E.W.: All right.

Ficino: *Still, why are you binding together immortal souls?*

P.G.:   I suppose Ficino is saying that Pico is forcing these great authors, immortal souls, into one book. They should not be compared and contrasted with each other as each one is unique and should be studied separately.

P.O.:   You don't know this though, it is your interpretation.

E.W.:   It does sound as if Ficino is criticising Pico to me.

Ficino: *I have been complaining about this very point before your Mithridates and also Pierleone.*

(Mithridates, a name given to a Hebrew scholar who worked with Pico and helped him on the translations of the Chaldaeic. He may have been sent to collect Ficino's work on Plotinus for Pico. Pierleone was another Greek scholar, physician to Lorenzo.)

Ficino: *It is not your (Pico's) particular genius I find fault with, rather your particular desire (cupidinem). I put my **work*** *before Mithridates.*

E.W.: *Cupidinem* also means lust or greed, Pico's greed, is desire strong enough here? Wouldn't greed be better?

P.O.: No, desire would be more accurate.

P.G.: It seems to me that these are not criticisms of Pico, they are instructions. Ficino is telling Pico to rely more on his own knowledge and not to try to accumulate it from outside, particularly when it is interfering with another man's work.

E.W.: But to the outside world these would appear to be criticisms and that is why he did not want this last part of the letter to be published, it would bring Pico's work into disrepute.

The letter finishes:

Ficino: *But I would not wish to introduce fortune when life should be governed by reason. And so my friend, may we live by reason. And let us as friends live with our lot in life. Farewell.* *Florence September 1486.*

P.O.: I'm still not happy with it, it sounds stilted. I would like to make some small alterations to the English, then it would flow better.

The group goes over the translation again quite quickly, the end result is now better. As always we feel that we could improve on it but decide to call a halt. There have been differences of opinion over the letter, P.O. is completely faithful to the text, P.G. finds this unacceptable if the meaning is obscured due to too great attention to detail. E.W. listens and understands both sides, but in the end reason and respect for each other prevail. Like Ficino and Pico, we remain friends. The letter will be beautifully written out and we will hear it again after an interval of a month as it will be easier to make any minor alterations when we are not so familiar with it.

It is Christmas time. We go downstairs to the Refectory and amongst a crowd of others we drink two strong glasses of mulled wine together. We wish each other a Merry Christmas and go home.

To sum up, the following have been the rewards of being a member of a translation group over the years:

The most obvious is that the skill in translating has improved, there is still the same uncertainty when first looking at a Latin sentence, there probably always will be, but the understanding comes more quickly. There has been an opportunity to spend weeks in the country pursuing the practice of translating in good company, that is, not only the company of friends but in the company of a master teacher, Ficino; it is a privilege to listen to his words as he would have spoken them, to translate them and contemplate them. The translation process remains a mystery, characterised by no perception of passing time or of an individual or of a group. Great ideas are considered and there is an inner certainty when close to the truth of a sentence or a letter. When I read the letters which we are supposed to have translated in the past, I cannot for the life of me remember what part of the letter I translated, no memory now remains at all of that work and, even if I wanted to, I could not claim what I have done for I cannot remember what I did. Is anything left at the end of the day? Certainly, the same person who started to translate Letter 15 Volume 1 all those years ago is exactly the same person who is writing this article now, but the purpose has changed, I now translate to gain a greater insight into myself, and really discover in practice what is meant when Ficino says:

If each of us, essentially, is that which is greatest within us, which always remains the same and by which we understand ourselves, then certainly the soul is the man himself and the body but his shadow.

Marsilio Ficino:
Magus and Cultural Visionary

THOMAS MOORE

*The philosopher knowledgeable about natural objects and
stars is appropriately called a Magus. With special lures
he introduces celestial things into earthly at the proper
times, just as a farmer skilled in grafting puts a fresh
branch into an old stump.* *

WHEN I first came across the writings of Marsilio Ficino around 1972,
I had no idea that this man who lived in another era would have such
an impact on my life and work. When I found Ficino, little of his
writing was available in English. I had some Latin from my years in a
monastery, but I found his language and his ideas difficult to follow.
His word order seems to have been determined by a shuffle of papers
or random selection. Still, amid all the knots and omissions in the
dense pages of his writing, I found an extraordinary worldview.

What immediately attracted me was Ficino's blending of theology,
philosophy, music, medicine, therapy, astrology, and magic. My image
of the Renaissance was one of scientific discovery, the humanism based
on appreciation of classical literature, and the flowering of the arts.
What I found in Ficino was even more interesting and fundamental.
He was proposing an alternative to a rationalistic approach to daily
life. Along the way, he was also reconciling paganism and Christianity–
an extraordinary accomplishment. Most inspiring to me, he presented
the image of the magus as the ideal figure to heal our wounds, both
physical and psychological.

*Ficino, *The Book of Life,* ch.26

As the passage I cite above puts it, the philosopher who has the special knowledge and skill to connect the celestial to the mundane is properly a magus. I had yet before me, in 1972, almost twenty years of practice as a psychotherapist, but even then I was interested in a therapeutic approach to things. I have never been a pure intellectual, and academia quite rightly invited me out of their circle after I had taught in my own way for a number of years. Ficino, too, seems to have had a therapeutic stance and was not part of the academic scene of his time.

Epicurean Therapeutics

Today the therapeutic point of view can appear bothersome to academics because it is so engaged with life and its intellectual basis is often slight. A large number of research studies joined to a list of techniques do not add up to an idea about human living. Often in modern therapy there appears a gaping whole where real thought might be expected. Therapy is also often materialistic, full of unspoken agendas and norms, and vague about purpose.

But the therapeutic position of Ficino is much more interesting and grounded. He is concerned about how to live a fascinating and creative life. His three books on life, *De vita triplici*, are self-help books of a particular kind. They tell you how to dress, what to eat, when to make medicines, where to live, which music to listen to, how to decorate your home, and how to read. When I first began publishing my own books on soul, which are heavily influenced by Ficino, I was compared to authors who give advice on food preparation, home decor, and party preparation. This comparison was a way, of course, to make little of my writing, but as far as it went it was accurate. I have learned from Ficino something about the spirituality of everyday life.

Even now it is difficult for me to explain the difference between superficial, bourgeois attention to manners and Ficino's insight that the spiritual life of the soul is fully contained in the details of everyday living. We live in a time when the spirit is automatically identified as transcendent, sublime, and upward. It is not easy for the modern person to imagine the spirituality contained in fashion or cooking.

Early on, the historians say, Ficino was an Epicurean, though he later rejected this philosophy. His essay on pleasure scans the long history of the idea, but adds little new reflection. Still, throughout his writing, especially in his emphasis on the qualities associated with the planets Sol, Venus and Jupiter, we find that his Epicureanism is much in evidence. For example, he recommends making wine in autumn, baking bread daily, and making gourmet feasts when the stars are most beneficent. His Epicureanism is not the materialistic philosophy of atoms but rather an acknowledgment of the importance of deep pleasure.

Ficino's attention to the details of everyday life is a facet of his Epicureanism, and in a sense his therapeutic goal is the Epicurean one of relieving pain and advancing substantive pleasures. He doesn't write much about fixing things that need repair. He never explains any human problem in terms of childhood trauma. But he does advocate a way of life that is full, rich, and multidimensional.

In his attention to the stuff of daily life he is also reconciling the highly spiritual and often ascetic Christianity with the more mundane spirituality of classical paganism. He sees a constant connection between the profoundly archetypal, spiritual, or celestial and the most concrete details of life on earth. The philosopher magus, he says, is one who knows how to bring the remotely spiritual into the mundane the way a farmer grafts a fresh branch onto an existing stump. This kind of philosopher knows nature very well, and he also knows how to draw the spiritual life into the mundane as a way of nurturing the soul.

The Mediating Soul

The first sentence of Ficino that I read was one that struck me so powerfully that I included a photograph of it from an old edition of *De Vita* as the frontispiece of my book on Ficino. Here are the key sentences as they appear at the opening of the first chapter of Book Three:

If there were only two things in the world, the mind and the body, without a soul, then the mind would not be connected to the body. It is immobile and entirely lacking in affect. It has no way of moving, and it is very far removed from the body. Nor would the body be connected to the mind, because it cannot move by itself. It is completely powerless and itself far removed from the mind. But if the soul is placed between them and is adjusted to each of them, then there is easy congress between one and the other.

To some extent, all my work since has been centred around these few sentences. The question is, how to place soul between mind and body, or between rationality and physical existence, so that our lives will be intelligent and sensual, our sensuous, practical lives will have meaning, and our quest for understanding will be full of life and relevant to everyday concerns.

Here we have a new definition of the therapeutic enterprise: a way to make sense of life and live it fully. The way, Ficino makes as clear as can be, is to cultivate the soul as an intermediate factor. The life of the soul will be connected fully to sensuous living and to rational thinking. But the soul will have its own way of connecting to each. Thinking might be sensuous, poetic, grounded, full of imagery. Physical life will be soulful–brimming with value, beauty, pleasure, art. I get these extensions of Ficino's meaning directly from his writing, especially as it is spelled out in the remaining pages of *De vita*.

Yet another aspect of Ficino's Epicureanism and a signal of what he means practically by giving the soul a role midway between the intellectual and the pragmatic life is his emphasis on friendship. The style in his letters may seem florid in comparison to modern taste, but his expressions of affection sound genuine. Epicurus taught the importance of friendship and listed it as one of the deep pleasures. Ficino thinks it is one of the most important things in life. In a letter to his friend Francesco Tedaldi he says, 'Attend to me to whom you are as dear as the dearest.'

He also advises Francesco not to travel too much. 'Think less about leaving your sons good things than giving them good company,' he writes. Ficino himself had a large correspondence but didn't travel much. One historian called him the least active person in history. Travel and activity are works of the spirit, and, according to Ficino's crucial paradigm, such spirited endeavours can leave soul in the dust. Care of the soul might require staying home, being with friends, and remaining in the company of your family.

So we find that Ficino's approach to philosophy is not at all the abstract analysis typical in our time. It's true that in his writings he continually surveys the history of philosophy and theology, but he always comes back to daily living. He is a practical philosopher, the kind with whom you might make an appointment to discuss the values being expressed in your daily life. This, by the way, would be an intriguing possibility in contemporary life–to leave behind the tightly circumscribed world of psychology for a practical application of philosophy.

Art and the Magus

In my own recent work I have been emphasizing a Ficinian style of caring for the soul, which I believe is the core of his practical philosophy. But equally fascinating is his vision of art. The elaborate theory of images contained in the third book of *De vita*, based on passages in Plotinus and the Hermetic texts, could seem quaint and absurdly irrelevant in the modem world, more appropriate for the forgotten culture of magic than for these enlightenment times. But just a little reflection and licence with interpretation makes them highly relevant and applicable.

The theory in brief is this: Each of the planets contains a particular spiritual quality which shines down on our earthly setting in the form of rays. This planetary radiance is like food for the soul and is important in its variety and particularity. In other words, we need a good spectrum of all these rays–Mercurial, Saturnine, Venusian, and so on–in our persons and in our environment. In our daily lives we have two ways to attract, capture, and absorb this radiance. We can find those things in nature that attract the various spirits and use these things when we sense a need for their special spirit. Alternatively, we can make things carefully so that through their character they will attract certain radiances the soul needs. To Ficino, works of art and craft are decoys or lures drawing certain spiritual qualities deep into their substance. This idea is familiar in many religions where a holy statue or icon is seen as the residence of a deity or spirit, and the literature sometimes points out that when the statue is particularly well made, the spirit cannot help but be drawn into it.

The implications of this theory are fascinating. Art, culture, and even fashion and decorating are not about self-expression or political agendas, nor are they meaningless and superficial enterprises. The purpose of art is to provide a society and individuals with the soul nourishment of particular kinds of spirit made available through images, music, architecture, and all the other arts and crafts. The way you design and furnish your house is an important part of soul care and has everything to do with the condition of the soul life of the family, the marriage, and the individuals living there. The same applies, of course, to the work environment or to the public domain.

I find in this theory of soul nurturance the basis for a new approach to the arts, to psychology, and to public life. The arts are of prime importance to the soul. When a culture is set up neglectful of the soul or, as is often the case, completely oblivious to it, then the arts fall into decline because they have no reason for being. They are aimless and marginalized. But once you introduce the soul into your concerns, especially with Ficino's paradigm in mind, then the arts take centre place.

An art work is not an intellectual statement, certainly not a puzzle to be deciphered, and its primary reference is not the artist, not even the artist's unconscious. In the Ficinian paradigm the artist is quite seriously a magus, one who knows nature–human and otherwise–and can find the spiritualities that are hidden within natural things and images. The artist-magus can also make images that entice the spirits we need into them and then invite us to expose ourselves to these much needed spirits.

Modern psychology tends to be focused on the individual person, as it looks for solutions to personal problems through behaviour adjustments, analysis of personal history, and drugs. A Ficinian psychology recognizes that one's entire current environment–the home, workplace, geographical location, natural setting, and public works– are all profoundly involved in the psychology of individuals and communities. Care of the soul is as much attention to the making of culture as it is care for the individual's everyday, concrete life and certainly more than adjusting the personality.

Finally, a soul-centred theory of culture recognizes that public life, including highways, politics, public buildings, economics, and entertainment, is also central to the soul's life. In a sense, we are what we build. If we build purely functional buildings for the exclusive purpose of efficiency and productivity, we will be persons filled with the spirits of efficiency and productivity and nothing else. If we want to be beautiful, we have to make a beautiful world and surround ourselves with the beauties of nature. If we want to be friendly people, we need to have friendly roads, bridges, and food markets. The soul is not wholly interior and not at all wholly personal and individual. The soul is communal as well, and its community includes objects, animals, and the things of nature.

Ficino's vision is an ecological one, not in the limited sense of preserving the natural environment, but in the more embracing sense of making the whole of life a home (*oikos*) in which we can live soulfully. The primary purpose of human life is an ecological one: feeding the soul by making a spiritually alive culture.

Spirituality in Ficino is not only the transcendent kind focused on higher consciousness and the perfection of the person and the world. It is a world spirituality, where spirit is made accessible through the sensuous things of life. In Ficino we find a thorough reconciliation of the transcendent and the mundane in his approach to the very meaning of spirit. Some of this spiritual work is accorded to the priest, but the rest is in the domain of the magus, and ultimately it may not be possible to distinguish the work of the priest from that of the Ficinian magus.

It is crucial to remember that Ficino's soul culture cannot be fabricated from the essentially narcissistic, personalistic, and rationalistic point of view characteristic of our time. Just as Ficino turned to Plato and Plotinus and their ilk for a fundamentally alternative philosophy, eschewing Aristotle and the mechanistic universe, so we need a fundamental shift in philosophical base. I think the image of the magus could be the fulcrum for this change. Our role is not to psychoanalyze and rationalize, building a culture based on our analyses, but rather to work magic.

Our buildings could be magical images, more powerful in their impact on the soul than for their capacity for work. Culture could feed us with its beauty rather than simply give us space for the application of our rationalizations. To the magus, the things of nature and human creativity are not part of a world that is split between thought and concrete existence. Every object shimmers with fantasy and addresses the soul. It is the very work of the magus to perceive the inner life of things and employ them in the making of a culture that fundamentally cares for the soul as its primary reason for being.

Marsilio Ficino and Medicine

CHARLOTTE MENDES DA COSTA

*I have read in Homer that one man of medicine is worth a
host of other men and justly so; for the sacred writings of the
Hebrews teach that the power of healing is the gift of God,
rather than an invention of man. Let us honour the man of
medicine because the Almighty created him of necessity.* *

To UNDERSTAND Ficino's works on medicine, it is necessary to appreciate his perspective that the health and long life offered by the art of medicine was to be used in the service of God and mankind.

The above quotation is from a letter by Ficino entitled 'The nobility, usefulness and practice of medicine'. The very title shows the high regard Ficino had for the Art. It also shows his practice of referring everything to the ultimate Good, that is God, as the source of all goodness. Ficino is often to remind us of the Father of Medicine, Apollo, represented as the Sun, and also the god of music, poetry and prophecy. In another letter he states that the subject of the art is Man, declared by Hermes Trismegistus to be virtually the greatest of gods, after Almighty God.[1] Also that everything on earth and the cosmos itself is there for the sake of Man. Thus the science of caring for Man is the most perfect. No physician should say that his art is caring for the body alone since the care of the soul and of the body come together in one.

Though it is unlikely that Ficino ever qualified in medicine, he did train to be a doctor at the University of Florence and possibly Bologna, under a certain Professor Niccolo Tignosi of Foligno. The biographers and his writings show that he practised medicine, certainly at Santa

* Ficino *Letters*, Vol. 1, letter 81

Maria Nuova, then the largest hospital in Florence. Ficino's father, Diotifeci was a doctor and had wanted his son to follow in his footsteps. He had been the physician to Cosimo de'Medici. One of the reasons Ficino gives for writing his main treatise on medicine, *Three Books on Life*, was to repay his Father. Ficino claimed he had two fathers, Ficino the doctor and Cosimo de'Medici, his spiritual father[2]. He was ordained a priest in 1473. He was also in touch with some of the leading Florentine physicians of the day, some of whom he addresses in his letters.

Ficino's medical traditions were based on Hippocrates, Aristotle and Galen, as translated by the Arab writers Averroes and Avicenna. He would have learnt the humoral system and that astrology and medicine were inextricably linked. Both medicine and astrology relied on the four elements air, fire, earth, water. The corresponding four humours or bodily fluids were blood (sanguine), yellow bile (choler), black bile and phlegm. These humours had the qualities of warm and moist, warm and dry, cold and dry, cold and moist. The best temperament consisted of a good measure of these four humours. The Galenic system was used well into the 19th century. Disease was usually seen as a consequence of a loss of balance in opposing qualities.

Ficino's writings on medicine are found in his letters, the *Three Books on Life*, and his *Consiglio contro alla pestilenza*, a work concerning control and treatment of the plague. The letters are inspiring eulogies, treating of the glorious future of medicine and praising both its divinity and utility.

De Triplici Vita

But what in fact if it is not an empty sign that Bacchus happened to fall from my lips just now? For perhaps he really heals more soundly with his nourishing wine and carefree jollity than Phoebus with his herbs and his sacred chants.[3]

De Triplici Vita (The Three Books on Life) constitutes Marsilio Ficino's great work on medicine. In the proem to the edition that combined the works, which Ficino dedicated to Lorenzo de Medici, Ficino names Bacchus as the deity presiding over the work. Ficino, a doctor and son of a doctor, wrote for scholars like himself, kindred spirits. He suffered ill health throughout his life and was particularly prone to melancholy. His decision to begin by exalting Bacchus as the God representing not only carefree jollity but also spiritual regeneration is illustrative of Ficino's kaleidoscopic and yet pragmatic approach to medical science, which is in some ways very modern. *De Vita* was very popular during the Renaissance, running to nearly 30 editions, the last being 1647, nearly 150 years after Ficino death.

This was, as Ficino rightly says, the first treatise to consider the health and illnesses of intellectuals. It may well be still the only such book. Today it may be considered a sub-specialty of Occupational Medicine. What does Ficino really mean by a scholar, or an intellectual? He could at one level mean students or academics, but he seems rather to refer to all people with great aims in life, those people who he says are yearning for knowledge, who are prudent, temperate and likely to benefit mankind in the public or private domain.[4] In book two, these men are described as deserving of a long life.[5]

Those young and old, exhausted in the pursuit of Minerva, Ficino exhorted to approach him as a physician and he will dispense advice and remedies to assist them in their purpose. These books he says are not written for ignorant, lazy people or the wicked and unjust: the drones as opposed to the bees.[6]

The three books are: Book 1 'On a Healthy Life' Book 2 'On a Long Life' and Book 3 'On obtaining a life from the heavens'.

De Vita: Book 1

In Book 1 Ficino prescribes a regime for scholars. They need to take care of their brain, heart, liver and stomach in the same way as athletes take care of their legs, as these are the instruments of their trade. They are particularly susceptible to black bile and phlegm and must scrupulously avoid them. Black bile produces melancholy or depression while phlegm is more suffocating to the mind. Ficino emphasises the positive aspect of the former by saying that it can be useful if not too extreme, and that it is the physical basis for the type of madness which is genius. This is asserted by Plato and Aristotle.

So it can seem to lead to creativity and wisdom, though in excess may produce mania or profound depression. What exactly is black bile? The answer is not clear, though it may lie in the area of psychiatry and disturbances of neurotransmitters, the substances in the central nervous system which allow signals to be transmitted between nerve cells. Ficino's doctrine of melancholy as expressed in Book One had far reaching effects on subsequent (English) literature, in Colet, Spencer and Burton's *Anatomy of Melancholy*. Some of Shakespeare's characters, Hamlet and Jacques for example express these traits. The turn of the twentieth century saw attention focused on this divine, prophetic type of madness as a source for creative genius. Today there are correlations between certain kinds of psychopathologies, mainly manic depression, and creative achievements in individuals with exceptional creative abilities. These include musicians, composers, writers, artists, Nobel laureates and so on.

The main causes put forward by Ficino for melancholy in scholars are 'celestial, natural and human.'[6] They tend to come under the influence of the planets Saturn and Mercury. Scholars can spend too much time contemplating, take too little exercise and have poor digestion. Other occupational hazards of scholars are headaches, poor vision and insomnia. In humoral terms they become cold and dry. Much of Book One is spent giving directions to counteract the effects of black bile and phlegm, dealing in detail with pharmacology and regimen. Ficino always advocates prevention of disease before speaking of a cure.

The regimental advice, diet and otherwise is often common sense. For example, sleep at night, rise early, study or meditate early in the morning, do not study later than noon. Exercise twice daily. Eat moderately. Avoid excessive sexual intercourse. Some of the compounds mentioned have recipes unknown to us and even some plants are rather obscure. Modern knowledge of pharmacology and toxicology would preclude some of the medicines given especially those of precious stones and metals. However many of the herbs are used for the same purposes by herbalists today, and also in some proprietary medicines. For example fennel was used by Ficino against phlegm, today it is used to aid digestion and as an expectorant. Marjoram is to be used for headache, rubbed over the forehead and temples; it has the same use today.

De Vita: Book 2

In Book 2 of *De Vita* Ficino concerns himself with the subject of how to live a long and healthy life. This he says is necessary so that one may perfect one's knowledge. He is certain that it is not just fate which determines the life's length but that one may lengthen it by effort.[7] However, before one rushes to find the elixir of life he gives the caveat, as spoken of earlier that this knowledge is only for good men who want to benefit mankind in whatever way appropriate. In fact there is no *elixir vitae*. There is, as in Book One, more advice on diet, way of life and some prescriptions for medicines. Much of the book is based on the humoral system: difficult for us to comprehend from the standpoint of Western medicine today.

For example, the heat should be kept in proportion to the moisture, the blood and moisture should be airy and tempered but also firm in substance.[8] So, one avoids excessive watery foods like fruit and takes olive oil. Similarities with this Galenic medicine may be found in the *Ayurvedic* (ancient Indian) and Chinese systems, still much in use, and popular today. All Chinese doctors are trained in traditional Chinese and Western medicine. Simplistically, diseases are explained as imbalances in elements or humours, and people's temperaments are described similarly, thus allowing treatments to correct the imbalances.

The dietary regimen again is on the whole sensible, as in Book One, although some advice is different from today: for example, limit the fluid intake (wine or otherwise). The diet should not be too strict, vegetarian is preferable. Eat according to the season. Select the best produce, the finest wheat and wine. Ficino, the doctor, would disapprove of modern intensive farming methods, as he advocates crop rotation, cultivating leguminous plants between crops, as opposed to putting manure on the fields. It is now known that intensive farming depletes the soil of minerals and trace elements, producing less nutritious crops.

There is also advice concerning care for the elderly. By elderly Ficino means those over fifty! They should dwell in sunny places in the winter, among green plants; eat honey, nuts, dried fruits and warming spices, and also live with healthy people. The spirit should be nourished with odours and fresh air. Bacchus and Phoebus are again mentioned; to preserve youth imitate both Gods. To imitate Bacchus, take to the hills, drink wine, worry not; for Phoebus, take in sunlight, sweet herbs and listen to good music. Above all pray for a long life so that one may live for the human race and for God.[9]

De Vita: Book 3

Book Three, 'On obtaining Life from the Heavens' is the most philosophical, mystical book of *De Vita* and is devoted to the use of astrology in ones life and medicine. It is also in part a commentary on some of the works of Plotinus. To understand the book better and find it practical one would need to be well versed in astrology and be prepared to try it. Despite all this, there are some useful conclusions which can be drawn from this book although one does need an open mind.

The premise on which this book is based is that of the macrocosm within the microcosm, that Man's nature contains all the qualities and powers of the heavenly bodies. The heavens are said to be truly alive, a perfect body revolving in perfect motion:

> These celestial bodies are not to be sought by us outside in some other place; for the heavens in their entirety are within us, in whom the light of life and the origin of heaven dwell.[10]

The individual nature of Man varies according to the positions of the heavens at his birth, hence a natal chart can be drawn up for each person. However the essence of Book Three is that a man may strengthen his natural powers by attracting favours from the heavens, in the imitation and openness to the particular planets, not by their worship. Ficino highly recommends that an individual finds his ruling planet which promised him good at his nativity, and begs favours from it.

Which qualities arise from which planets? Detailed astrology is not within the scope of this article but one could summarise:

Sun   – intelligence, pursuit of truth, honour
Jupiter   – the laws, temperance, philosophy
Mars   – movement, magnanimity, aggression

Venus   – love, gaiety

Mercury – eloquence, ingenuity

Moon   – procreation, life, life of plants

Saturn   – stability, perserverence, agriculture, one set apart, blessed or miserable.

Ficino allows us to 'assume a virtue if you have it not' (Shakespeare) and points the way heavenward.

From every star hangs a series of things under its dominion: animals, plants, metals, gems, and the superior i.e. the star, draws to itself what is inferior in the chains of beings. For example the lodestone, or a magnet, turns towards the pole star, flowers turn towards the sun. In order to obtain gifts from the celestial bodies our spirit should be prepared by using the appropriate medicines, odours, songs, foods, even contemplations and thoughts. These gifts are strengthened if this preparation is at auspicious times. So for example if you want to receive power from the sun, find those solar types of metals, gems, plants, minerals, like gold, myrrh, frankincense, heliotrope plants, cinnamon, and use appropriately. One should think solar thoughts, keep company with solar types of people, and get a lot of light. This should all be at times when the Sun is well aspected. Through particular behaviours and thoughts we are quickly exposed to those planets which signify the same affects.

Ficino speaks of the power of music and song. Harmonious music, through the influence of the planets, has the power to calm and move our spirit. All music arises from Apollo, hence its healing powers, but it may pertain to other planets. Of use would be Jovial, Venereal and Mercurial types of music. Music for celestial benefit was practised by the ancients: the Pythagoreans, the Hebrews. Literature throughout the ages is full of the praise of music, as a manipulator of emotions. Take for example *Samuel* 7.23:

And it came to pass when the evil spirit from God was upon Saul, that David took an harp, and played with his hand, and so Saul was refreshed, and the evil spirit departed from him.

In *Romeo and Juliet* IV, 5 we find:

When griping grief the heart doth wound
And doleful dumps the mind oppress,
Then music with her silver sound
With speedy help doth lend redress.

Today there are good associations with music and medicine – as exemplified in music therapy to relieve mental illness and stress. Many doctors, too are skilled musicians.

Obtaining life from the heavens may seem at first glance a rather strange, occult book on astrology with no relevance to us today. It is worth noting that Ficino's knowledge came from ancient sources: the Greeks, Egyptians, Chaldeans all of whom could make precise astronomical predictions. It would be easy to ignore a work like this because it does not fit into our mechanistic, logical framework. However if it does work, one can imagine the uses astronomy might have in preventive medicine and in strengthening existing (modern) therapeutics, by methods outlined in Book 3.

By remembering that all the qualities of the heavens are within us, that 'Our passions are celestial influences already planted within us,'[11] we can utilise those qualities if only by contemplation. Another piece of advice is useful:

To live well and prosper know your natural bent, your natal star, your genius and what place is most suitable to live. Follow your natural profession.[12]

De Vita was not without controversy at its publication, chiefly over the third book. It brought Ficino into direct conflict with the Church because of its use of astrology, magic, talismans, and apparent advocation of worshipping other Gods. Ficino himself answers any criticisms both within the book and in an *Apology* afterwards. He says categorically that astrology should not derogate from the worship of the one God or detract from one's free will.[13] He cites ancient doctors as being priests and astronomers. He also advises us to read the book impartially. He admits that he does not much approve of the use of images or talismans but recounts their uses in the course of a commentary on Plotinus.

Consiglio Contro Alle Pestilenza

Ficino's work on the plague, *Consiglio contro alle pestilenza*,[14] was printed in 1481, in response to the plague which ravaged Florence from 1478 – 1482. It appears to have been used as a plague tract well into the seventeenth century. Ficino shows the astrological portents for the plague (retrospectively), the conjunctions of Mars with Saturn in the 'human constellations'. He presents the causes as this and poisonous vapours, the usual causes proposed at the time for epidemics of this sort. Preventive measures include fleeing the city, avoiding the places of contagion and the body and personal effects of persons killed by the epidemic - all sound advice. Interestingly he gives no place for prayer or meditation to prevent or cure the plague. The cures include the traditional Theriac, and plague pills with diverse recipes, as well as surgical remedies of the plague boils.

The Doctor and the Holistic Approach to Medicine

It is good to examine further Ficino's views on the doctor, medicine as a healing art, and its highest aspirations. His sublime writing could inspire any modern doctor, even the overburdened, overworked, 'burnt-out' doctor one hears about today. Without good health, Ficino says, little can be achieved and little enjoyed. Good health is almost a prerequisite to living a good life.

> The doctor should remember that the creator of health is God, that nature is God's instrument for establishing or maintaining health, and that the doctor is the servant of both.[15]

For Ficino, a doctor must have devotion to God and charity towards men as well as a keen mind, knowledge and experience. The doctor prepares the ground and removes the obstacles so that nature may do the healing. In general, diet and exercise should be the principle means of cure. Drugs of all sorts should be avoided. This agrees in part with modern medicine and patients' views. Doctors prefer not to write prescriptions and try to avoid unwanted side effects of drugs, if possible. Doctors hold a revered place in society, since by their care and dedication a good life may be sustained. The status of the doctor today is slipping and as a result respect is lost. There is a self-deprecating tendency in the medical profession today when ethical or moral issues arise. There is a fear of being seen to be proud, paternalistic and full of self-knowledge. Ficino insists that a doctor must be a man of principle and virtue. Juxtaposing the modern trend with the stand Ficino takes, raises interesting questions.

Ficino gives the ultimate aim of medicine. This is, that the doctor prescribes for the good of all people, caring for the life and prosperity of the individual and for humanity. While Galen was doctor of the body, Plato doctor of the soul, Christ himself was the ultimate healer of bodies and souls, the doctor of mankind who gave the power of healing to his disciples. In a letter speaking of the medicine for the ills of the world, Ficino says that nowhere is there found a medicine adequate for the earthly diseases, except divine love and worship; a far stronger medicine is needed which is spiritual and above the world.[16] This theme is hinted at throughout *De Vita* and underlies it.

Though today most doctors would deny their role in caring for men's souls and might well deny man a soul at all, they do recommend counselling to clear a patient's emotional problems. Few doctors could deny that many patients come with emotional or mental difficulties as either their presenting complaint, or masquerading as a physical complaint, or exacerbating a physical illness, for example stress worsening high blood pressure. Depression and other mental illnesses are endemic within our society. Prozac and other antidepressant drugs are not the whole answer. In General Practice, the doctor as priest role is talked about, but few directions ever given.

Faith and trust in the doctor is an important part of the healing process and conducive to health for the sick person.[17] This is a view current today. Patients often remark that they feel better after seeing the doctor even if no prescription is given. A good relationship between patient and doctor is most important for the patient's trust and subsequent well-being, this is well known. This faith may be responsible for the placebo response (medicine given to humour rather than cure a patient). The placebo response is a therapeutic effect as a result of this 'humouring', maximised by the doctor's empathy and the patient's trust. The beneficial results of such a response from a doctor has been confirmed by research.[18]

Of further relevance today is Ficino's view of man as having a mind-body continuum.

> It is wrong to cherish only the slave of the soul, the body, and to neglect the soul, the lord and ruler of the body, especially since the Magi and Plato assert that the entire body depends upon the soul in such a way that if the soul is not well, the body cannot be well.[19]

He understands Man to have a physical body, a mind, spirit, soul and intelligence. Although different parts of the soul and body are addressed, he never loses sight of the whole. Western medicine today draws its understanding of health and disease from detailed descriptions of physical conditions while largely ignoring the mind. Even higher cognitive functions and emotions are put down to workings of the brain alone. Ficino seems to understand how the physical affects the subtle and vice versa. For example, to avoid black bile, avoid dry, stale, salty foods and avoid anger, fear, sorrow; take walks by rivers and keep agreeable company.[20] Taking the topical example of meditation, some insurance companies have offered reductions of health insurance premiums by 30% if there is proof that a person is meditating regularly.[21]

Ficino's views on prayer and meditation are undergoing a resurgence of popularity. It is interesting that faith *per se*, faith in God, is according to a recent study from Duke University, North Carolina, productive of a difference in longevity and good health in those who attended Church regularly and those who did not. Out of 4,000 over-65-year-olds studied for six years, those who attended Church at least once a week had a forty per cent lower blood pressure than those who did not, significantly lowering their risk of heart disease and stroke.[22]

Ficino gives an example of how prayer helped himself during an illness and also how a boy with a severe head injury under the care of Ficino's father recovered when the parents of the boy offered prayers to the Virgin Mary.[23] There are modern studies on this theme. For example the work of Dr Randolph Byrd at San Francisco General Hospital in 1988 showed that of two random groups of 393 patients in a coronary care unit, ignorant of the experiment, those in the group who were supported by intercessory prayer showed a markedly less severe illness course.[24]

What does Ficino mean by health? He certainly means a healthy mind and a healthy body. He often speaks of the doctor-priests of old, of the Egyptians, Chaldeans and Persians, and the Magi who were physicians of the soul and body. The Magi thought that the mind of the sick should first be cleansed with sacred teachings and prayers before they attended to the body. Ficino shows that many wise and ancient men have practised medicine and gives its splendid genealogy, from a God, Apollo, through heroes, kings, leaders, Magi and philosophers. He quotes Cornelius Celsus (first century AD) when he says that the art of medicine was understood when one could comprehend the movements of the mind and body, and Avicenna (980 - 1037 AD) who judged that the body exerted strong influence on the mind and the dispositions of the mind exerted the greatest influence over the health, good or bad of the body. Care of the soul Ficino judged to be of greater importance than care of the body but that bodily health should not be neglected.

Conclusion

What would be Ficino's advice for doctors today, what sort of doctor would he be? Much of his writings are timeless, applicable across the ages. A doctor will always need knowledge and experience, and to take profound care of his patients. No doubt he would now write within the framework of modern medicine today. One must remember that in the Renaissance era, the Galenic system was the only system doctors knew. Today we really know little about that system and explain disease in the physical pathologies as far as we know. Ficino would certainly praise and use the enormous body of scientific research largely from the last two centuries, giving us the breadth of medical knowledge we are so fortunate to have today. One cannot ignore this knowledge, and any of us, faced with a serious illness would doubtless want the best treatment medicine has to offer. We might also want a doctor who cared for our soul and had a holistic perspective. That this is what patients want is shown in the enormous rise in complementary therapy, whether practised by doctors or other medical practitioners.[25] There is no reason why a good doctor should not combine the best medical treatments with care for the soul.

As an example Ficino says that serious music maintains and restores harmony to parts of the soul while medicine restores harmony to the parts of the body. Since the body and soul correspond with each other it is easy to care for the harmony of both in one man. Some say that the case for mind-body medicine and a holistic perspective of health is unscientific, intuitive and unfounded but in fact there is a large body of scientific knowledge accumulating which supports this view, confirming the intuitive, philosophical knowledge of a man like Ficino.

Returning to Bacchus, good humour affects health in a positive way, laughter reduces physical and emotional tension, increases the ability to cope with pain and stimulates the immune system.

The arrival of a good clown exercises more beneficial influences on the health of a town than twenty asses laden with drugs.
Dr Thomas Sydenham, 17th century physician

A merry heart doeth good like a medicine: but a broken spirit drieth the bones.
Proverbs 17.22

Ficino was keen for us to realise this. He advises us to live joyfully, in the present, day by day and not to worry about one's present circumstances or the future. Finally he says do not be too diligent in caring for one's health. Freedom from care and tranquility of mind are necessary for life.

'*Laetitia coelum vos servabit vestra.*'

'By your own joy, heaven will preserve you.'

NOTES
1. *The Letters of Marsilio Ficino*, translated by members of the Language Department of the School of Economic Science, London. Vol 5.14
2. *Three Books on Life* trans. by C.Kaske & J.R.Clark, published by Medieval & Renaissance texts & studies, New York, 1989, Proem.
3. *Ibid*, Proem
4. *Ibid*, Book 1.I
5. *Ibid*, Book 2.II
6. *Ibid*, Book 1.IV
7. *Ibid*, Book 2.I
8. *Ibid*, Book 2.IV
9. *Ibid*, Book 2.XX
10. *Letters*, Vol 4, 46
11. *Three Books on Life*, Book 3.XX
12. *Ibid*, Book 3.XXIII
13. *Ibid*, Book 3. XXV
14. *Marsilio Ficino's* Consiglio contro alle pestelenza *in the European tradition*, Paul Russell, May 1998
15. *Letters*, Vol 1, 81
16. *Letters*, Vol 5, 4
17. *Three Books on Life*, Book 3.XX
18. Black F. 'Harnessing Placebo Power', *Current Therapeutics* Nov.1991:84-85
19. *Three Books on Life*, Book I.XXVI
20. *Ibid*, Book 3.X
21. Orme-Johnson D: 'Medical care utilisation and the Transcendental Meditation Program', *Psychosomatic Med* 1987:49:493-507
22. *The Times*, 14.8.98
23. *Letters* Vol 1, 80
24. 'The Positive Therapeutic Effects of Intercessory Prayer in a Coronary Care Unit Population.' *South Med J*, 1988:81(7) 826-829.
25. Ernst E: 'Distrust me: I'm a doctor'. *British Journal of General Practice*. Sep.1998

Note in relation to references 18, 21 and 24 I have relied on summaries contained in a discussion paper entitled 'Stress and Illness and the Mind Body Connection'(1993) by Dr Steven Sommer, Senior Lecturer, Department of Community Medicine, Monash University, rather than on the content of the papers themselves.

A Little Lesson in 'Counter-Education'[1]

A Dialogue with the Ghost of Ficino on the Theme of Psychotherapy

NOEL COBB

The soul is the greatest of all miracles in nature. All other things beneath God are always oné single being, but the soul is all things together...Therefore it may rightly be called the centre of nature, the middle term of all things, the series of the world, the face of all, the bond and juncture of the universe. *

AFTER fumigations with sage and frankincense, I light two candles and place them in the antique silver, mock-Renaissance holders, the ones with the images of Saturn, Hermes and Aphrodite embossed on the stems. I set them carefully on the windowledge of my consulting room, overlooking the back gardens of my home in Hampstead. I think of Ficino's own house in the hills of Careggi which I visited in early May 1993, when we convened to celebrate his life and work in the nearby Villa Medici. I have heard that the old Marquessa, who owned the house and tended it like a shrine, has since died. But I have not heard what has happened to that hermitage-like house with its curtains of meditating silence, so shockingly perforated by sudden peacock screams. The visit there was intensely gripping, as if the rich Etruscan honeygold of the walls had brushed the depths of the soul, soaking it with shades of the deepest welcome. Unforgettable: to see Marsilio's carefully calligraphed words in neat sepia ink on a letter to a friend in 1466. And to read inside an early vellum-bound book set perhaps on

* Marsilio Ficino, *Theologia Platonica*[2]

181

one of the first miraculous Gutenberg presses: MARSILIVS FICINVS FLORENTINVS CVNCTISSEMEL EPISTOLIS SVIS.S... and in another: MARSILIO FICINO SOPRA LO AMORE O VER' CONVITO DI PLATONE...

NC: Dear Marsilio, how fortunate that your words have survived, and now, half a millennium later, new technologies can make translations of them available to the whole world! Your work has become a touchstone of basic sanity in the midst of a relentlessly greedy and violent world which seems bent on strangling the life of the soul and the spirit with its brutal insistence on a monotrack of materialism. Little father, where are you now? Your spirit was never more needed. Will you come to sit with me awhile at the end of this millennium, so similar to the end of your own century? Listen, I will play some chords for you on a lyre I have made from bulls' horns and a tortoise shell. Here's a golden fifth– and a third, a fifth again and now: a seventh, for dissonance's sake! *(hollow sounds of strummed lyre strings)*

MF: *(Faintly at first, as if from a long distance):* You call me...merged in blissful union...with the Muses...I have so little cohesion in your hungry world of shape and succulence...Yet, I mark your call for help. I will gather myself in order to speak with you. (pause) Yes, my last years were sorrowful. My patrons, Cosimo, Piero, Giuliano and Lorenzo gone; Pico, Bandini and Poliziano all departed. Savonarola preaching wretchedness and crying for the flames; the best minds lacking all conviction; corruption and deceit enthroned in halls of power...But it's always the same. How impure this world is, how illusory and how deceptive! What is real is in the invisible world; in the visible world is only the shadow of the real.

NC: Marsilio, I thank you for coming. I am going to make notes on everything you say – so that people may read it in a book which is to appear soon about you.

What I have so often wanted to ask you is: 'Where would you begin today if you were to educate our psychotherapists?' How would your 'counter-education' address our secular priesthood, particularly those smooth arbiters of reason and unreason, clever interpreters of dreams and unassailable abusers of Imagination? I'm sorry, I must explain: in our century a new 'profession' has been created for 'the care of the soul'; soon it will have 'respectable' status, registers of 'accreditation' and regular policing of standards and standardization of approach. It is called 'psychotherapy'–after the Greek (*psyche*= soul; *terapeutes*=giving care or attention to the divine)

MF: I do not understand. There can be no standardization with respect to the soul. All care of the soul must allow the Unknown, the Unforeseen, the miracles of poetic invention and spontaneous imagery– these things have their own rules, their own demands and requirements. None of this can be standardized; no one can be 'authorized' or 'accredited' to care for the soul. I suppose you are facing the same problem we did with the Academy. It is a perennial one. Who is truly worthy of being admitted to the company?

NC: Yes. But we have reached a peculiar situation– where an insidious rigidification, a fossilization, of the work has set in–and increasingly individuals with no real faith in the soul or creative genius or spark of daimonic intelligence embark on a 'training' in this new 'profession'. It is largely this level of mediocrity which gets the blessing of 'accreditation' from the training institutes. Alongside this we have a situation where madness is defined medically and specialist-doctors called 'psychiatrists' pretend to know what is mad and how to treat it, usually with chemicals designed to kill the madness but with the side-effect of often leaving the individual numb to himself and the world or lost in oblivion. In this way they lose touch with the individual who is suffering from their diagnosis. On top of that, all states of mental distress are now classified medically! The 'codified' states of unreason are given numbers in a diagnostic manual, to help practitioners identify them.

MF: As Sprenger and Kramer did for Pope Innocent the VIII when they devised that inquisitor's manual, *The Hammer of Witches* ... In my time, though, there were no such self-appointed 'professional' adjudicators of 'mental health', a law unto themselves. There were, of course, the priests–whose immediate appeal was to the Pope, but whose ultimate appeal was to God or the Holy Scriptures. That system was also open to corruption, but there were some quite active checks on the priesthood. These checks came from the polis, which means, 'the city' or 'the community'. The people would not listen to anyone for long who went against the needs of the soul. Eventually, the soul will be heard.

NC: That's just it. Maybe that isn't true any longer. We are approaching a system of psycho-social control so restrictive and self-referring that it completely *invalidates* all disagreement with it, under the pretence that it is benevolent and full of concern for the good of mankind. The definition of 'mental health' which it employs is so inflexible and mediocre that it is strangling the voice of the soul. Marsilio, we need your *divinely informed* imagination and wide generosity.

MF: I do believe that injustice and tyranny will be seen for what it is and, no matter how subtle and insidious, one day, will be overthrown. In Florence, even Savonarola–who tried to throw soul and beauty into the flames–was burnt at the stake himself in the end.

NC: So you believe that eventually things out of balance–like the current tyranny of the soul by professionalism and mercantilism–will be brought back into balance?

MF: Yes, the soul generates its own convulsions, its own revolutions and renewals. And– the citizens will not be duped forever.

NC: But, Marsilio, what should we, as therapists, be aiming for?

MF: First of all, you should aim to act as a *mediator* between the world of matter (the body, in the broadest sense of the word: the shared physical world we inhabit as incarnate beings) and the Divine. Like Plato's *Soul*, you should be a 'go-between'– connecting individual human beings with the archetypal realities of the *Nous*–or what your modern translators of Plato and Plotinus have called 'the Intelligible Realm' –which in turn is the ineffable exfoliation of the *One*.

NC: That's a tall order. Can you give us some idea of how we might do that in practice?

MF: I begin with the Heavens, then the stars, those cosmic *scintillae* or 'sparks'–which in reality are profound mind-forms comprising vast patterns of Being, distinct and innate structural templates for modalities of consciousness.

NC: Do you mean the zodiacal 'constellations'?

MF: Yes, I mean those awesome figures of light which revolve around the spatial 'spine' of our planet. Those 'constellations' are so real and un-arbitrary that even the tiniest birds, like Blackcaps or Garden Warblers, can use them to navigate during their noctunal migrations over thousands of miles. They can locate the Pole Star even when it is hidden by clouds, by extrapolating its direction from surrounding constellations! The same birds do this each year, arriving at the same tree in the same garden or field or wood which they nested in the year before. Ceaselessly moving through the band of the twelve ecliptic constellations are those seven Archons of our solar system, including the Sun and the Moon. I mean, Mercury, Mars, Venus, Jupiter and Saturn...I understand that your astronomers have found three more with your magnificent magnifiers of the skies.

NC: Yes, contemporary astrologers include what they call the 'outer' planets or the 'transpersonal planets': Uranus, Neptune and Pluto in their calculations of astrological questions.

MF: So they must. But for us in Medicean Florence there were only seven planets to reckon with. Saturn was the greatest and the most powerful, thus the most feared. I spent most of my life in fear and trembling over the power of Saturn, constantly imagining ways in which to mitigate his austere demands on me. As you know, this planet was the ruler of my horoscope, being conjunct the horizon and square to Mars at the time of my birth. Ultimately, though, I had to thank Saturn for forcing me to develop my own kind of 'psychotherapy'–my way of 'Living One's Life in Accord with the Heavens'–that's the title of 'Book Three' of my *Liber de Vita*, or *Book of Life*, directly inspired by Plotinus's *Ennead* 4.4. 30-42.

NC: So, you suggest that the therapist imitate the soul in the Platonic scheme of things, taking up a middle ground between the spirit and the body, mediating one to the other.

MF: Yes, that's it.

NC: And you maintain that it is also important for the therapist to be something of an astrologer?

MF: I do, but not the predictive, 'let's outwit fate' kind who swindles people by playing on their greed and insecurities. No, my kind of astrologer is one in whom there is a great devotion to, and respect for, this plurality of divine principles–a kind of polytheist of the soul; one who recognizes the distinct differentiations of the One. What I mean is: imagine a person who can teach us ways of tuning into the distinct frequencies of the planets. He knows how to 'attune himself', just as if he were a string instrument, to the 'vibrational rays' of the 'planets', creating beautiful 'music' through developing perfect 'pitch' and an understanding of the 'intervals' that create exquisite harmonies. He teaches this to those who come to him in distress because of the 'discord' in their lives. He teaches the artistry of life lived in accord with the Heavens!

NC: *'Discord'*–meaning that we suffer and do not bother to ask what the gods may wish of us and thus do not give to the gods what they demand? And further, that we suffer because we are not 'attuned to the Heavens'?

MF: Yes, that is exactly what I mean. You see, we are so used to a monotheistic theology that we have stopped being able to think differentiatedly about things. Of course, I am using monotheism and polytheism metaphorically. But look: if one does not see that there are various definitely differentiated kinds of energy in the universe, then one lives one's life blindly, unable to relate the conflicts and confusions in one's life to specific faces of divinity which, after all, are universal and involve everyone. And, returning to your concern for 'saving' madness, do not forget that the great Plato spoke of at least some kinds of madness as being 'gifts from heaven' and 'the channel by which we receive the greatest blessings'. Perhaps it is important for your 'therapists' to distinguish between 'divine' and 'ordinary' madness.

NC: Marsilio, that's wonderful! Listen, I would love to tell you about a kind of psychology which we have been developing in the past few years. It has grown out of a study some of us have made of your work. We call it 'archetypal' because the archetypal perspective provides a common connection between what goes on in any individual soul and what goes on in all people in all places in all times. It allows psychological understanding at a collective level. Archetypal, in other words, means fundamentally human. Those are the words of an inspired genius of our time, a teacher like yourself– who also respects the larger picture–an American psychologist called James Hillman. He loves your work and has called you the 'Renaissance patron of archetypal psychology'.

MF: I am glad to hear that my work has been taken up by imaginative thinkers in your era and applied to your world and its vicissitudes and not just relegated to historians who so often fail to bring their understanding to bear on the world of the present.

NC: Could we talk more about 'living one's life in accord with the Heavens'? As a therapist, I meet people of all ages, from many walks of life and in very different stages of understanding. They suffer from things as different as compulsive grinding of the teeth to intolerable attacks of spontaneous panic and inability to cope with this world's barbaric brutalities. They can be subject to horrific seizures of rage, states of suicidal loneliness, fears of howling distintegration, loss of all direction or interest in life. They often cannot love the persons nearest them. They are crushed by thoughts of total insecurity. They lack all trust in life and confidence in the future. They live lives of such complete dishonesty that nothing is real to them. They sink into such profound states of melancholy that they do not see the reason to go on living. It seems the psyche is endlessly prolific in its capacity to create disorder and illness and suffering in any aspect of its behaviour. Yet, it seems equally able to experience and imagine life through these deformed and tortured perspectives. When I was young I thought, following the dominant ideas of the time, that the way to 'treat' these disorders was to uncover the shocks and upsets in that person's family drama by a kind of *anamnesis* of childhood memories. But over the years, as I had more and more experience of life, I found that the literal re-living of terrible experiences and all the analysis of them never actually altered the person's present experience of the world– and if it did, it was invariably to flatten out all the nubs and wrinkles that gave that person any real character. I was convinced that there was something greater which needed to be re-collected. We needed to recollect our origins *beyond* the literal conception of this life.

MF: Yes, I see that you have 'returned' to the Platonic form of *anamnesis*, which means 're-calling or remembering one's *divine* origins, not confusing this with one's biological origins. Platonic anamnesis is a worthwhile kind of remembering to do, and if your psychotherapy, as you call it, can do this for an individual, then it is really on the right track. You know, it made an immense difference to me when I was able to see that my moods of black despair and despondency had their origins in Saturn. It was then that I realized that to serve a sickness was despicable and degrading to my humanity, but to serve a God was divine. I found that what was required of me was to begin to honour this Saturn who had such a prominent place in my nature.

NC: I have seen that individuals have a deep longing, usually not spoken about and usually hidden from the world out of embarrassment. This longing or yearning for something else, which they long to find again, is a form of archetypal nostalgia, a nostalgia for the archetypal, a homesickness for one's imaginal home, our Other Home, that home which is intangible and invisible, our soul's home in the stars, as Plato might say. It is this home and the memory of this place which Socrates is always leading his pupils towards. Children today are not encouraged to remember this Other Home, the Home that Plato says is our *true* origin, the one that the Sufi poets cry out for in pain. It is as if psychology has become completely materialistic and the only level of reality left is the literal one: my 'home' is the house I was born in or brought up in and my 'family' is my biological family. This is where our 'developmental psychology' locates itself–in the *literal* family and the linear, one-way development from infancy.

MF: This connects with something else: you mentioned taking a wrong turning in your career when you adopted the idea that the cause for someone's suffering lay in a literal event of their past. From my point of view no experience or event in our lives has at its roots a material cause. It is foolish to look for causes in the material world. Everything in this world has a spiritual cause. So, I must ask you if your approach adopts this attitude–that the suffering you meet in others has at root a spiritual cause.

NC: I'm glad you asked me that. I was fortunate enough to have been initiated into this work by a deeply spiritual woman who said to me that she believed that all of our psychological problems were in the end spiritual ones. She taught me to let go of the belief that one could find causes to present sufferings in literal events of the past. That was extremely radical and liberating. From that time I have never 'looked back', as it were. Not that I am not interested in the past, quite the contrary, but now I don't misuse it to shore up a collapsing theory of personality. I love looking at an individual's past, including their childhood–the whole life of a person is a wonder and a miracle of individuality. In particular, how the shaping of that individual with all its wondrous quirks and peculiar talents, begins already in earliest infancy.

MF: I wrote in some of my books about the ancient Greek idea of the *daimon*. I could not write too openly about it because I would have been in a lot of trouble with the Church. But among ourselves in the Academy we were very excited by its possibilities. Poliziano especially. I found it fascinated me–this idea of the genius or guardian spirit that accompanies us from birth. This idea alone is enough to make the vicissitudes of our lives understandable–and bearable!

NC: I think that this idea would have a profoundly liberating and healing effect on the 'profession' of psychotherapy!

MF: Most certainly! The old idea, the idea which was held by the pagan Greeks, was that 'each person enters the world *called*.' That idea is mentioned, for example, in Plato's *Myth of Er* at the end of his *Republic*. In a nutshell this idea says that the soul of each of us is given a unique daimon before we are born, and that it chose an image or pattern that we live on earth. This soul-companion, the daimon, guides us here; in the process of arrival, however, we forget all that took place and believe we come empty into this world. The daimon remembers what is in our image and belongs to our pattern, and *therefore our daimon is the carrier of our destiny*. A calling may be postponed, avoided, occasionally missed. It might also completely possess you. However, eventually it will out. It stakes its claim. The daimon doesn't go away.

According to Plotinus, we elected the the circumstances, the place, the parents and the body that suited the soul and that, as the myth says, *belong to its necessity*. This suggests that the circumstances, including my body and my parents whom I may curse, *are my soul's own choice*–and I do not understand this *because I have forgotten*.

If we see this myth as referring to the 'spiritual causes' I spoke of earlier, then *we must attend very carefully to childhood* to catch early glimpses of the daimon in action, to grasp its intentions and not block its way. There are some important practical implications that follow from this, especially for this 'care of the soul' of which you have been speaking: first, we would have to recognize 'the call' as a major fact of human existence; second, we would need to align life with it; third, we would have to understand that wounds, abuses, victimizations and all the seemingly pointless disasters of a life belong to the pattern of the image, are necessary to it, and help to fulfill it.[3]

NC: Marsilio, this would completely revolutionize our way of thinking about our lives! We would no longer be able to blame others, our family or our parents or the world, for things which have happened to us. We would have to accept responsibility for our own lives. When confronted with an unpleasant or traumatic experience we would have to ask ourselves, 'What does my daimon want of me; what is he trying to tell me?' not 'I have been seriously damaged and wounded by that unjust abuse and it is to blame for my being crippled and warped like this.'

If we start with the idea of the daimon, then we might perceive those 'terrible events' in life in other ways: as twists of fate designed by the daimon and intended to give one the kind of warp needed to make one into the kind of person capable of displaying that particular form of mad artistry or carrying that particular message out into the world– or, as initiations, initiations into peculiar styles of being which one would never develop otherwise. These pathologizings would not be seen as defects to be discarded, but emblems to be proudly borne. A sense of the heraldic, the mythical would be primary with us. We would bow in respect to the prolific pluralism of the World Soul's absolutely fantastic fecundity, ceaselessly creating more stunning, astonishing, wild, beautiful, unnecessary, feverish, hilarious, formidable, ferocious, lugubrious, entertaining, masterful, crepuscular, surreal manifestations of so-called human nature.

Is that why you urge us to study astrology? Can we come closer to this kind of understanding through looking at the way the stars configurate around an event?

MF: I see the planets as messengers of the Most High; Lords of the pluralistic universe. We did not create them. They are not an invention of ours. But we are of theirs!

There was an idea which I came across in the neo-Platonic thinkers I was translating when I wrote the *Book of Life*. I could not develop it as I would have liked because the watchdogs of the Church would have had me impaled on their sharp dogmas. But I can tell you, I was excited! Thinkers like Iamblicus clearly believed that the daimon existed in the train of a deity! That meant that there could be Saturnian daimons in the train of Saturn, Mercurial daimons in the train of Mercury or Venusian daimons in the train of Venus, and so on. Do you see the wonder of this! It meant that there was a way of *ordering* the apparently chaotic experiences and happenings around the daimon! A way of understanding them in relationship to the divine. You could apply this idea when attempting to make sense of a patient's particular sufferings– by asking yourself, to whom does this experience or event belong? Is it of a Saturnian nature? A Venusian nature? And what does the divine influx require now of that individual? Is it asking that he honour Saturn in accepting the melancholy fit that has fallen on him or that he honour Venus by paying more attention to beauty in his life? We need to stop asking how we can get what we want and begin asking what we can do to honour these divinities in our lives. For the pagans that was easy; they were always asking: 'What is it the Gods want of me?' The daimon is a mediator, too. A soul-figure. Through conversation with the daimon, I discover what is being asked of me. And the daimon connects me with the *Nous*, the spiritual reality of the cosmos, in which all things here below owe their origin and being.

NC: So, we are back at the begining: the circle come round: the soul as mediatrix and mediator.

MF: Yes, as Pico and I used to say to each other:

The soul is the greatest of all miracles in nature. All other things beneath God are always one single being, but the soul is all things together. It possesses the images of divine things on which it depends itself and the concepts and originals of the lower things which in a certain sense it produces itself. And since it is the centre of all things, it has the forces of all. Hence, it passes into all things. And, since it is the true connection of all things, it goes to the one without leaving the others. It goes into an individual thing and always deals with all. Therefore it may rightly be called the centre of nature, the middle term of all things, the series of the world, the face of all, the bond and juncture of the universe.

NC: One last question before you go– and thank you, Marsilio, for being so available to us when we need you–what I wanted to ask you was this: Looking at our world from the perspective of the immortals, do you feel that this world is worth bothering about, is it not just illusion and tedious toil? Should we not strive to leave it as soon as we are able?

MF: You sound as melancholy as I was in my life in the Cinquecento! I understand your longing for the eternal. And life in the world you inhabit and which I no longer do–yes, that life *is* an illusion, but a miraculous one. It's as though stardust had blown about the universe and then gathered itself together to form a consciousness-body, a body with which it could do all sorts of things: paint divine images, compose celestial music, dance heavenly numbers, construct architectonic dreams, devise ships that float on the sea and fly through the air, invent ways of turning lead into gold, carve beauty out of raw amorphousness, cook delicacies out of the greenery that grows out of the earth, make love in endlessly delightful variations and give birth to countless incarnations of the One...so many extraordinary ordinarinesses! So that the One can mirror itself in an infinity of images, exfoliating in ever-increasing intensities of involvement with the unformed, self-forgetting, losing itself in the miracle of the unforeseen and finding itself in the celebratory discovery of worlds without end. We are it, it is us! This entire world of so-called illusion is only the play of the One! Don't forget Plotinus's last words: 'Let us work to return the divine in ourselves to the divine in the All'...

I think that is all I want to say today...

NOTES

1. *cf.* Eugenio Garin, *Portraits from the Quattrocento*, trans. V.A.Velen, (New York, Harper & Row 1972). For example, (p153): 'Ficinian philosophizing is in essence only an invitation to see with the eyes of the soul, the soul of things...an incentive to plumb the depths of one's own soul so that the whole world may become clearer in the inner light.' and James Hillman, *Re-Visioning Psychology*, (New York, Harper & Row, 1975), p201: 'Ficino's invitation to see psychologically is a revolution in philosophy. Because of the centrality of soul, all thought has psychological implication and is soul-based...Philosophy is a psychological activity.' and: 'Therefore the ground of philosophical education becomes a reeducation in terms of soul. This in Ficino's eyes is a countereducation, or 'the introspection of an interior experience which teaches the independent existence of the psychic functioning.' (*Ibid*). For further discussion of 'internal experience', see the chapter by that name in: Paul Oscar Kristeller, *The Philosophy of Marsilio Ficino,* (Gloucester, Mass., Peter Smith, 1943/64).

2. Marsilio Ficino in the *Theologia Platonica, Op. Om.*, p121; quoted by Kristeller, *Ibid*, 120.

3. For a rich development of this theme, see J. Hillman, *The Soul's Code*, (New York, Harper & Row, 1996).

Marsilio Ficino on Leadership

DAVID BODDY

Love of mankind alone is the food by which men are won,
and only by the favour of men do human affairs prosper. *

THERE is a crisis in leadership in the world. Political and business leaders are suffering the burdens of office, facing turbulent changes in both social and economic systems, and all without an apparent reference to an unchanging authority, either in their own lives, or when taking decisions in public office.

Real leaders never move from the single authority of the will of God, which shows itself as both love and law. Lawful living is conducive to consciousness and wisdom, and such living is naturally full of love. Love and law are two forces generally absent from current considerations of public affairs, yet for Ficino they were the very essence of the matter.

As philosopher and priest Ficino was obviously well qualified to expound, through the beautiful poetry of his letters to many of the key decision-makers of the day, the reverence of God and its practical application in the meeting of secular and religious conspiracies and other events. As a consequence of his single focus on the divine, it would be all too easy in our modern world of tabloid newspaper headlines and media soundbites to discard his advice as irrelevant. Yet deeper penetration of his advice, along with a willingness to use human intelligence to discover universal principle and apply it to particular and current situations, would bring rich rewards to contemporary business and political leaders.

* Ficino, *Letters*, Vol 4, letter 27

Ficino perfected the art of providing hard-hitting advice, including to souls whose high station in life was put on them by others. No modern 'spin doctor' or management consultant would dare take up the position of speaking as Truth herself, yet Ficino in his advice to the very young Cardinal Riario on the education of a ruler, does just that. As he tells the 16-year-old, thrust into high ecclesiastical office by his uncle, Pope Sixtus IV, 'let her [Truth] earnestly entreat you to hear her awhile with a generous mind, as she speaks out for your benefit, for she may not know that you always hear her willingly; to hear anything in any other way is erroneous and unprofitable.'[1] How wise to position the adviser so as not to let the messenger be shot, the fate of too many well-meaning political and business advisers when the client did not like the advice, (for how can Truth be tied to a stake?); how wise, too, to call out the best in the listener, for the best is nothing but Truth itself.

This was perhaps Ficino's finest gift: his capacity never to separate himself off from those to whom he was speaking. For this reason, Ficino could discourse on affairs of Church, State, business, family, marriage, the stars, medicine, and all manner of worldly issues. His real knowledge came not from books, but from Himself, which was no other than the Self he was talking to. He merely held up a mirror allowing those with eyes to see and those with ears to hear. His purpose was to be a reflector of divine wisdom.

To those engaged in worldly affairs he gave emphasis to the importance of duty. In correspondence with Cherubino Quarquagli, a grammarian, musician and poet who was an early member of the Academy, he sent advice on the duties of the priests, the judiciary, the merchants, the private citizen and other sectors of the community. Given a contemporary setting, it sizzles with scalpel-like precision, but a distinct lack of political correctness.[2]

To the clergy he says: 'The virtue and duty of a priest are a wisdom that glows with piety, and a piety that shines with wisdom.' In reference to men struggling with their sexuality he says: 'A man should beware of being effeminate in any way.' Church leaders rent asunder by doctrinal dispute and behavioural inconsistency could take note.

To the judiciary he reminds them that: 'The duty of the magistrate is to remember that he is not the master but the servant of the law, and the public guardian of the state; furthermore, that while he is judging men he is being judged by God.' With European legal systems vying for supremacy, and banks of unaccountable judges sitting forming laws on human rights, as if God had not already done so, such advice is worth remembering.

Could the scandals of the Robert Maxwell pension funds, or the Japanese banks, or the American home loans fiascos, or the countless other cases of commercial corruption, hurting millions of people across the world, have been changed if Ficino's guidance to merchants had been heard and followed? He says simply: '[The duty] of the merchant, with true faith and diligence [is] to nourish both the state and himself with goods from abroad... Merchants should so seek wealth that they harm no one. For whatever arises from evil in the end falls back into evil. Let them keep their wealth in such a way that they do not seem to have acquired it in vain, nor just for the sake of keeping it. Let them so spend that they may long be able to spend, and may prove to have spent honestly and usefully.'

Not with the eye of prophecy, but with the voice of understanding, he alerts both politicians and businessmen to the inevitability of economic cycles; and to stockbrokers he encourages a longer-term outlook, not a short-term fix. 'The fortunate man should understand that the good things of fortune are good only to the good man; and that after fair weather, comes the rain. The unfortunate man should reflect that the evil that fortune brings is evil only to the evil man, and after days of rain he should expect fair weather. For we see that Spring restores to the trees the leaves that Winter took away.' Of course it begs the question: who is the fortunate man; and who is the unfortunate?

An issue bedevilling business success today is the relation between employer and employee. Corporate barons too easily set themselves apart from the most intelligent asset in their service, the people who work for them. Too easily the divisions increase, and the work force clutches at the tail of 'democracy' to try and achieve rights which, if employers understood the love and respect which is due to the humanity in everyone, would not be needed. Loyalty to an employer is at a premium, and for those whose skills are in highest demand and who can move with ease from job to job, nearly non-existent. The costs to commerce and industry in overcoming these problems are huge. How would Ficino approach this?

When speaking to the young Cardinal Riario, he said: 'Remember that your servants [employees] are men, equal to you in origin, and that the human species, which is by nature free, ought not to be, indeed cannot be, united by any fear, but only by love.'[3]

And how should employers speak to and act with their employees? 'Just as almost all men of power delight in their several possessions, neatly disposed and displayed in their homes, so will you delight in a mind that is ordered by fine language and conduct.' And what should they learn at business school? 'It will be your art to temper both the desires of the mind and all your actions lest, when all external things are in harmony for you, the mind alone be in discord. It will also be your schooling to make frequent study of the most select writers, lest the mind alone be impoverished in the midst of such great riches.' It hardly needs saying that neither the works of Plato, nor the Bible, feature on the top-ten business books list, yet Ficino is adamant that those men who seek to rule over others should surpass those they lead in wisdom. The proposition is undeniable, but to embrace it would cause serious revision to virtually every MBA course, along with serious denting of business-guru egos.

Conduct in both public and private of our leaders has always been an issue. Can good government seriously be achieved when men of high office proclaim for political ends certain values, yet live in private by entirely different standards? Ficino warns the young Cardinal: 'No great man ought to believe that his conduct can in any way be hidden. For the greatest things, whatever they be, are most fully exposed to view and are the envy of all who forgive little and disparage much. Since it is very difficult for a prince to conceal himself from others, let him see that nothing at all lies hidden either in private or in public life.' As many fallen leaders would testify, when reflecting ruefully on their mistakes, it is not just the error that created the difficulty, but the cover-up.

So how should leaders behave? 'It is neither proper nor safe that one who should be watching over many men, and who is being watched by still more men, should ever go completely to sleep, or that the leader of many, by serving greed and lust, should become slave to a beast.'

'Let your mind be at once humble and exalted, a blend of dignity and courtesy; may you live temperately and speak truthfully, but sparingly. May you be generous in giving but not rash in promising. May you be firm in faith, your vision wide. May your judgements stand the test of time, following carefully the words of the wise. Lest many men should find it easy to deceive you every day, do not trust many and do not trust easily. Let not smooth persuasion or vain speculation move you, but nothing less than sure reason. Do not make a start on anything unless you have first seen that the end is both good and well-assured. Avoid servants who are evil or of ill repute, lest you yourself be reputed an evil master.'

By holding up a mirror, reflecting with clarity and simplicity the Will of the divine, Ficino serves mankind with wisdom, a mark of which is to stand the test of time. In relation to the history of mankind itself, five hundred years is a mere yesterday. Have we, as members of the human family, made in the image of God, endowed with love and reason, advanced in dignity, in humility, in true knowledge, since those glorious yet stormy days of the 15th century? How is it that we can develop technology, allowing us to communicate across the globe in an instant, and yet continue to mis-understand each other, dispute with each other, never really meet each other?

Ficino is not a man of the past. Some would argue, with good cause, that the wisdom he reflects is at least as pertinent today, in meeting our modern dilemmas, as it was when the Florentine ruler, Lorenzo de'Medici, was grappling with the inner-contradictions of his own soul. The icons in our society may appear to be different from those of former times and our willingness to stand for God and truth may appear to be weaker.

But it was not the masses that produced a Renaissance; it was the leaders. They turned to ancient wisdom. They studied and learnt. They practised, and had the courage to refresh that wisdom in a manner appropriate to time and place. Guided by the philosophers, like Ficino, the leaders were uplifted, by having their minds and hearts lifted towards God.

Our challenge today is to create the conditions which allow a new Ficino to arise; for those, gifted with the privilege of leadership, to let our human institutions shine with 'the eye of prudence, the scales of justice, the seat of fortitude.'

'Love of mankind alone is the food by which men are won, and only by the favour of men do human affairs prosper.'

NOTES
1. *Letters*, Vol 4, letter 27
2. *Letters*, Vol 2, letter 53
3. *Letters*, Vol 4, letter 27

Ficino's Message to the Church Today

PETER SERRACINO-INGLOTT

*Christ himself, giver of life, who entrusted the care of all
sufferers to his disciples, enjoins his priests, if they are no
longer able to cure with words as those of the past were,
then at least to provide therapy with herbs and stones.* *

THUS, on the 15 September 1489, in a letter of self-defence to three
eminent friends, wrote the Very Reverend Father Marsilio Ficino,
Canon of the Cathedral of Florence, in which high ecclesiastical post
he had been installed two years previously.

Thus, he proved himself to be one of the few outstanding priests and
prelates of the Catholic Church, except for missionaries in the field, to
have taken very seriously and literally the words of Christ as transmitted
in the Gospels, to the effect that the essential mission of His disciples –
that is the essential ministry of the Church – consisted indissolubly of two
things: to proclaim the good news *and* to cure the sick.

Ficino's notion of the priesthood – with its focus on holistic curing
of the human being, since body is related to soul, in the vision of this
arch-Platonist, as shadow is to body – certainly deserves closer scrutiny
from a theological point of view than it would be suitable to give it in
the present context. It is only being cited here as a striking instance of his
more general 'missiologic' concept of the Church in relation to the world.

This mission-centred concept took shape in Ficino's mind and heart,
no doubt in part because of the wider opening of intellectual horizons
and readier acceptance of the contributions of cultures other than those
of Judeo-Christianity as synthesized in the Middle Ages, that was

*Ficino, *Apologia, Opera,* p.573

characteristic of the early Renaissance in Florence. That context evidently gave a particular flavour to Ficino's thinking as a priest and gives it a great relevance to our time when the Church has to come to terms with the process of globalization, which has become the most impressive phenomenon of the last years of the twentieth century.

In this brief essay, I shall only try to indicate the great interest at this moment, when there is so much talk of 'a paradigm shift in theology', of just five key concepts of Ficino's thought – viz. *prisca theologia* and *preparatio evangelica, pia philosophia, theologia poetica* and *pax fidei*.

First, from the very first days of the diffusion of Christianity after Pentecost, two radically different attitudes towards previously existing religions appeared. These contrasting viewpoints were to crystallize later in attitudes such as those, on the one hand, of Tertullian, who regarded all non-Christian religions as works of the Evil one, and of many others on the other hand, ranging from St. Paul to Clement of Alexandria who evidently thought of other religions as somehow positively related to Christianity.

The contrast was to reappear sharply later, after the Renaissance, when the Church resumed its missionary activity after the sort of self-enclosure and stasis of the Middle Ages, in the opposed attitudes of St. Francis Xavier smashing the 'idols' and his fellow Jesuits, Matteo Ricci and de Nobili adopting Confucian and Hindu rites and language into a Christian context. It was not until the second Vatican Council, (1961-1965) that the Church was officially to endorse the second positive approach. Even so, it cannot be said that complete consensus has been attained as to the nature of the relationship between other religions and Christianity.

Ficino canvasses at least two theories in this regard. The first is that of *prisca theologia*. For instance, in the dedication of *De Christiana Religione* (1474) to Lorenzo de Medici, Ficino speaks of the 'eternal wisdom of God' as having been in the beginning 'wedded to religion'.[1] But he suggests that this original revelation of God by Himself was well-preserved in the Judaeo-Christian tradition, but not so well elsewhere. So there was an 'old theology' which had, over time, become more or less corrupted.

Secondly, however, in the same work (Chap. XXIV), Ficino gives a much more positive account of pagan religion. He considers that it constituted a *preparatio evangelica* among the pagans, as Eusebius had shown that Hebrew prophecy had constituted among the Hebrews. He outlines the role which the Sybils (even in today's Roman Catholic Mass for the Dead, in the *Dies Irae* sequence, we sing: *Teste David cum Sibylla*), Hermes and Virgil play in parallel to that of the Hebrew prophets. Whatever the historical and other scholarly inaccuracies which Ficino may have committed, his general argument, that the great minds of antiquity, and Plato above all, had forged concepts and related religious experience in language which proved to be just as important as those of the Hebrew prophets in the formation of Christian discourse, is plainly irrefutable. It is noteworthy that the late Professor R.C. Zaehner of Oxford University worked out a thorough account of the development of Hindu thought with regard to Christianity, in terms of its 'mystical' rather than its 'prophetic' content, parallel to the account which Ficino developed of the relationship of Platonism to Christianity.

Thirdly, even more interesting in this connection is Ficino's concept of *pia philosophia*, that is of the identification of a specific mystical tradition which links Hermes Trismegisthos (placed by Ficino on the same level as Moses, deemed to be his contemporary) to both Zoroaster Magus (identified with the Biblical Balaam) and to a genealogical line which proceeds from Orpheus to Plato. However unacceptable to modern scholarship some details of Ficino's hypothesized network may be, yet he was putting his finger on a very important historical truth, the importance of which is hardly ever underlined. All the monastic tradition of Christianity, in both the Byzantine and Latin branches of the Church is derived not from Hebrew or Biblical sources (where there is nothing resembling monasticism) but from Indian, Hindu and Buddhist, sources. Ficino perceived the Oriental origin of the 'mystical' element which developed together with the 'prophetical' element, as the Hebrew heritage of Christianity may be called. He could not, with the resources at his disposal at the time, figure out the media of transmission quite accurately. Relatively recent scholars have identified as key nodes in the network which relayed the *pia philosophia*, as Ficino called it: the meeting of Alexander the Great (in *c.*327 B.C.) with the so-called *gymnosophistai*, Yogi devotees of Shiva, in the region of the most Eastern ramifications of the Indus river; the journey to India by Panthenus, who founded the theological school of Alexandria, upon his return, in 180 A.D., and who became the teacher of Clement of Alexandria; and above all, Ananda Saccas, apparently a Buddhist monk, who became the teacher both of Origen, rightly called the first systematic theologian of Christianity, and the main source of Byzantine theology, and also of Plotinus, whom Ficino recognises as the main transmitter of *pia philosophia* to the West, largely through St. Augustine, main source of all subsequent Latin theology and, through his rule, of the Western monastic tradition. So permeated by Eastern-sourced spirituality were those times in Western Christendom, that in Migne's collection of the writings of the Fathers, a Mahayana Buddhist text is attributed to St. John Chrysostom[2] and a work on Brahmin traditions is attributed to St. Ambrose.[3] Ficino may not have been quite right in naming the sources of the *pia philosophia* but he was certainly right in discerning both its presence and its importance for contemplative life in the Church.

Fourthly, Ficino developed the concept of *theologia poetica* or 'poetic theology' which essentially consists in pagan myths read and interpreted in the light of Christ. Thus, just to quote one crude instance, the three goddesses between whom a mortal has to choose the most beautiful, represent the Contemplative, the Active and the Voluptuous lives, according to Ficino. The real depth of Ficino's reading of the myths could not really be appreciated before Freud and Jung had shown that the myths expressed deep psychological truths. Ficino, although he was unarmed with psychoanalytic techniques, and occasionally produces crude allegorical interpretations, on other occasions comes up with complex and subtle readings which could be compared to those produced in our own times by Eugen Drewerman, certainly one of the most brilliant Biblical interpreters of the twentieth century.

Finally, Ficino proposed what he called the *pax fidei*, essentially a process of reconciliation between the sons of Abraham, father of all monotheists, Jews, Christians and Muslims. Ficino realised that the first Christians never really intended to separate themselves from the Jews, and that Islam was nothing but a simplification of the Judeo-Christian tradition, for the sake of an essentially merchant people. Moreover, he recognises that there was a 'Platonic' – that is a Plotinian – mystical current – a *pia philosophia* present among all three of the prophetic monotheist traditions. Consequently, the same type of spirituality emerged among all three, and it constitutes the ground on which Ficino projected the scheme foreshadowing what has come to be called, after the Vatican Council, the 'wider ecumenism'.

Ficino's treatment of the subject can be profitably compared to that of St. Thomas Aquinas. The latter's *Contra Gentiles* is listed among the two works by Aquinas (the other being the small early pamphlet *De Ente et Essentia*) which Ficino 'owned'. The *Contra Gentiles* is Aquinas' defence of Christianity against the Jews and the Muslims considered in the constrained horizons of the Middle Ages as the only significant rivals of Christianity. Ficino altered the nature of this genre of writing in at least three important ways. First, the substance of the content is an attempt not so much at polemical confrontation, as rather at eirenic reconciliation. Secondly, this change of spirit is reflected in the chosen literary format, which abandons the antithetical structure of the medieval *Summa*. Thirdly, the religious dynasty of Jews, Christians and Muslims is seen in the wider context of universal religion.

At a stage in history when the Church, having played a notable role in bringing about the end of the Cold War and the East-West divide, is being confronted with theories of an inevitable 'clash of civilizations' between North and South, or Islam and the U.S.-led world, Ficino's concept of the *pax fidei* acquires extraordinary significance, especially if one recalls that he was writing at a time when fear of an Islamic superpower in the Mediterranean was haunting many minds. Obviously, the present context is different in many respects. Ficino does not provide a recipe for thoughtless application, but a deep orientation that is perhaps the only viable one to a 'peace of faith' Here again, Ficino figures, I believe, as an unacknowledged precursor in the formulation of much needed Christian concepts and attitudes in the world of today.

Ficino's call to the priesthood was what would be labelled today a 'late vocation'; he was ordained in 1473, at the age of forty. But it would be a mistake to think of it in either of two ways in which many historians present it. It was not a dramatic, Damascus-road type of conversion (from pagan Platonism to orthodox Christianity) and there are no traces of 'twice-born' style in Ficino. Nor, on the other hand, was it a spiritually insignificant step taken out of some petty motive, or in the throes of psychological depression.

For Ficino, there was a continuity between Platonism and Christianity as there had been for St. Augustine 'whose divine footsteps I frequently follow as far as I am able'[4], wrote Ficino. There was no deep conflict between Plato and Christ, for both Augustine and Ficino, for one good reason: both interpreted Plato and Christ equally in the light of the Plotinian account of mystical experience. Paul Henry, S.J., in his classic study *La Vision d'Ostie* has shown how Plotinus constitutes the literary infrastructure of Augustine's account of his conversion. Paul Kristeller has suggested that it was Ficino who has been described as reading Plotinus from the priest's place near the altar, in the Church of St. Mary of the Angels, in 1487; at any rate, the episode is emblematic of Ficino's attitude[5].

That Ficino took his priestly vocation very seriously emerges not only implicitly from such facts as his intensive writing of his book, *The Christian Religion*, for publication a year after his ordination, and of the *Commentary on the Epistles of St. Paul*, a year before his death, but also from his explicit statements on the subject.

'Holy Orders', Ficino wrote to Cardinal Riario, 'do not arise from the caprice of fortune, but from the eternal wisdom of God'[6]. It seems clear that, as Eugenio Garin has written, 'Ficino wanted to be ordained a priest, precisely to re-affirm the convergence of philosophy andreligion.'[7]

In fact, although Ficino explicitly argues in his letters that the Platonic idea of the philosopher-king was feasible, yet he gave much more importance to the idea which he himself derived from Plato, namely that of the philosopher-priest. The works of Plato to which he devoted most attention were, of course, the *Symposium* and the *Phaedrus*, where the central themes are love and the ladder of knowledge, by which it is possible to ascend to the world of eternal Being, rather than those in which politics is central. Plato himself was, for Ficino, an exemplar of the philosopher-priest, although that may not be the picture of Plato which contemporary historians mostly entertain.

Priests, including quite a number of Ficino's fellow-members of the metropolitan Cathedral Chapter of Florence as well as San Lorenzo constituted a well-defined category of members of Ficino's Platonic Academy. An essential function of the Academy as conceived by Ficino was that of bringing to faith in God those who had become atheists because of philosophic reasons. Ficino often appealed to his fellow-priests to strengthen their piety by means of the pursuit of wisdom, that is mainly by studying Plato.

Perhaps the most characteristic feature of Ficino's ideal of the priest-philosopher was that he should be proficient not only in theology and medicine (as noted at the beginning of this essay) but also in music. This requirement stemmed from the fact that Ficino did not consider the human being to be made up only of body and soul, but also (following Plato and Augustine) as comprising a third element, the spirit. To the spirit, music (and aroma) was what medicine was to the body, and the mysteries of theology to the soul. Ficino wrote in a letter to Francesco Musano da Iesi[8] (whom he had cured from a feverish disease) that, as in ancient Egypt, priests practised medicine, the lyre and religious rites, so too should any 'complete' human being today. Certainly, Ficino himself did all three. Admittedly, one consequence was that he was accused of being a magician. But that accusation, in turn , won for us Ficino's apologia, of which I began this essay with an extract, for his holistic concept of tripartite man - image of the Trinitarian God - and his extremely striking characterisation of the priesthood - at a time when many priests are suffering from a crisis ofidentity.

NOTES

1. Ficinus Marsilius: *Opera Omnia*, 2 vols., Basle, 1576, I, p.1.
2. Migne: Patrologiae Graecae, XCVI, 859-1246
3. *Ibid.*: Patrologiae Latinae, XVII, 1131-1146
4. Language Department of the School of Economic Science: *The Letters of Marsilio Ficino*, Vol. 2, London, 1978, Shepheard-Walwyn, p.28.
5. Garin E.: 'Marsilio Ficino e il Ritorno de Platone' in Garfagnini G.C. ed.: *Marsilio Ficino e il Ritorno di Platone, studi e documenti*, 2 vols., Florence, 1986, Istituto Nazionale di Studi sul Rinascimento, p. 11-12.
6. Language Department of the School of Economic Science: *TheLetters of Marsilio Ficino*, Vol. 4, London, 1988, Shepheard-Walwyn, p.38.
7. Garin E.: 'Marsilio Ficino e il Ritorno de Platone' in Garfagnini G.C. ed.: *Marsilio Ficino e il Ritorno di Platone, studi e documenti*, 2 vols., Florence, 1986, Istituto Nazionale di Studi sul Rinascimento, p. 10.
8. *Ibid.*: Vol. 1, p.39-40

Further Reading

'While I am reading your books, I live...' wrote John Colet to Marsilio Ficino. The best entry into Ficino's mind, and the easiest – as he himself intended – is to read his inspirational *Letters*. Apart from the individual volumes, there is a selection from the first five books of the English translation under the title *Meditations on the Soul* in which the letters are grouped by theme.

The works which inspired Colet, Erasmus, More, and many others are the *Theologia Platonica* and *De Christiana Religione*; while the *Timaeus* commentary is a mighty work in itself. The work which inspired, nearly a century later, Spenser, Sidney, Shakespeare and others was the *De Amore* – Ficino's commentary on the *Symposium* of Plato and a work in its own right.

As to Ficino's own vast reading, which would keep most of us busy for many years, the most-thumbed volumes on his bookshelf along with the Greek and Latin *Bibles* would have included Plato's *Dialogues*; St. Augustine's various works including the *Confessions*, *City of God* and *Soliloquies*; Mercurius (Hermes) Trismegistus' *Divine Pimander* and *Asclepius*; Plotinus' *Enneads*; pseudo-Dionysius; Proclus; Iamblicus; and certainly in mind, all of Aristotle's surviving works–which come in for less direct mention in Ficino's writings since he and all his readers were well grounded in Aristotle's systematic thought and wide-ranging investigations into the created world.

For Ficino's life, a full biography is still awaited at the time of writing; but the introductions to the volumes of the *Letters*, and that to *Meditations On the Soul*, will provide essential information. Professor Kristeller, whose lifelong devotion to Ficino has been a major factor in rekindling 20th century interest, provides a succinct evaluation of Ficino's significance in his Preface to Volume 1 of the *Letters*; an

209

evaluation which he re-states in 16 pages in his *Marsilio Ficino and His Work After Five Hundred Years*.

That this same volume devotes nearly 200 subsequent pages to a bibliography of Ficino, of which 30 pages consist of a list of books and articles about Ficino, indicates the very considerable scholarly attention given to Ficino in the latter half of the 20th century. Kristeller's two volumes of essays on *Renaissance Thought* are relevant; and his *The Philosophy of Marsilio Ficino* is a full-length study in depth of all the crucial concepts in their historical and conscious aspects. This is followed up in Michael Allen' s distinguished books and essays.

To this list of recommendations should be added the contributions to the several international conferences which marked Ficino's quincentenary year when these are eventually printed. The texts of the lectures to the 1999 international Ficino conference in London are to be published in 2000.

For a general background to the Renaissance, Vincent Cronin's two books, The *Florentine Renaissance* and *The Flowering of the Renaissance*, are readable, informative, and perceptive. For those curious as to the state of the learned mind in England during Ficino's lifetime, *Humanism and England During the Fifteenth Century* by Roberto Weiss is packed with scholarship and fluently written. Frederic Seebohm's *The Oxford Reformers*, though now a century old, is a revelatory account of the effect of Ficino's vision on Colet, Erasmus, and More around 1499.

The period just before Ficino's adulthood is covered by George Holmes' *The Florentine Enlightenment 1400 -1450*.

Two handy paperbacks for reference are the *Dictionary of the Italian Renaissance* edited (with characteristic touches of warmth and humour) by John Hale, distinguished Renaissance scholar and author of several other relevant volumes; and *Renaissance Philosophy*, by Brian Copenhaver and Charles Schmitt, a work of comprehensive authority, which includes a hefty 70-page bibliography, for even further reading.

It might be useful at this point to survey the state of English translation of Ficino's major works. Scholars have noted for many years now - whilst general knowledge of Latin has continued, to decline

- that for a just appreciation of Ficino's thought, students of philosophy and theology were poorly served in respect of Ficino's major writings in English translation.

As has already been mentioned, the *Theologia Platonica* (its full title continuing 'On the Immortality of Souls') is the fullest exposition of Ficino's thought. An English translation with annotation is due in 2000. The companion or balancing work, *De Christiana Religione* is in course of translation.

Ficino's commentaries attached to his own Latin translations of Plato's dialogues have been enormously influential over the centuries. Of these, the commentary on the *Symposium* (*De Amore*) has been translated into English by Sears Jayne - though out of print at the moment of writing. The *Timaeus* commentary awaits translation. Michael Allen has translated the commentaries on the *Philebus*, the *Phaedrus* and the *Sophist*. The rest of the commentaries - of varying length - still await translation.

Also awaiting translation is Ficino's commentary on Plotinus' *Enneads* - of particular interest since it is one of Ficino's later works; also the commentaries on the *Epistles* of St. Paul, and on the works of pseudo-Dionysius, both of which attracted the attention of John Colet.

The *De Vita Libri Tres* has been translated. as *Three Books on Life* by C. Kaske and J. Clarke; and the inspirational *Letters* arc slowly emerging in their twelve books via a team translation.

But there is much pure gold to be found in Ficino's shorter works, all of them written for a particular requirement; the Latin texts of most are to be found in the *Opera Omnia*, others in the *Suplementum Ficinianum* containing Professor Kristeller's discoveries.

Hopefully, this 'Ficino 500' year will spur commissions and translations and scholarly annotators. The situation should thus change from year to year; interested parties are recommended to write to the publishers for an update on this.

Perhaps the most practical celebration of Ficino's quincentenary would be to remedy the situation described above with a world-wide commitment to take on the translation and annotation of all of Ficino's' works.

The Contributors

Adrian Bertoluzzi has been a researcher for the textual and biographical notes of the English edition of the letters of Marsilio Ficino since its inception. He is working towards a biography of Ficino.

Clement Salaman is the editor of the English translation of *The Letters of Marsilio Ficino*, and also one of the translators of a new translation of the *Corpus Hermeticum*, entitled *The Way of Hermes*. He has taught classical subjects and history for over 20 years at St.James School for Boys, now at Twickenham.

Arthur Farndell's childhood awareness of the universality of truth and a glimpse during adolescence of the unity underlying the multifarious languages of mankind have led him to study philosophy and to help make available in English the words of a man who lived his life in the beauty of holiness.

Linda Proud is the author of *A Tabernacle for the Sun*, a novel inspired by the *Primavera*. It was in a book on Botticelli, studied in the early 1970s, that she first met Ficino and Poliziano - the two guides to truth, one philosophical, one literary, that she was to adopt for life.

Valery Rees has been a member of the team translating the Ficino Letters since 1976, but it was not until 1980 that she began her 'real apprenticeship', teaching Latin for 17 years at St. James School. A family holiday in Hungary in 1991 sparked her interest in Ficino's relationship with the court of King Matthias, and since then, returning to her earlier training in history, she has been pursuing research on this theme. She has published several articles in the UK and Europe, and organised the Marsilio Ficino Quincentenary Conference in London, 1999.

Dr. Joseph Milne is Research Associate of the International Institute of India Studies, Fellow of the Temenos Academy, and visiting lecturer at the University of Kent at Canterbury in the Department of Theology and Religious Studies. His particular interests are Christian Platonism, Eastern and Western mysticism, and philosophical anthropology. He also lectures on Ficino and Shakespeare.

Geoffrey Pearce has studied philosophy, history, and Eastern and Western astrology for over 30 years. He is a member of the American Council of Vedic Astrology, and Treasurer of the British Association for Vedic Astrology.

Dr. Pamela Tudor-Craig F.S.A. is an art historian who looks over the fences of specialisation. She ranges over time spans as wide as the eleventh to the eighteenth centuries. She likes to question the silences of the visual arts with the voice of literature, and to illustrate literature with the visual arts. As for music, she agrees with Ficino: it is nearest to the divine.

Jenifer Capper, with a degree in Classics and as teacher of Classics for the last fifteen years, decided to start looking at the curricula of the fifteenth century, where the great English education had laid its foundations. This led her to Vives; to John Colet, Dean of St. Paul's; and brought her back to Ficino, the translator of the Platonic dialogues, who enabled these men to have access to the thought of fifth century BC Athens.

Jill Line, M.A. (Shakespeare Institute, University of Birmingham) has taught Shakespeare for many years, most recently in the Drama department of the Roehampton Institute. She now writes and lectures on Shakespeare and Christian-Platonism and has written a series of essays on Shakespeare and Ficino for the Globe Theatre's season of Roman plays. She is a lecturer for the Temenos Academy.

John Stewart Allitt has for much of his life studied the art, literature and music of Italy, where he has lived; in particular, he has worked for the revival and understanding of Mayr and Donizetti. Like both these composers, he has found the world of Dante to be an inexhaustible treasury of knowledge and insight.

Leslie Blake is a barrister, author and lecturer on constitutional and legal matters. His most recent book is *The Prince and the Professor* (Shepheard-Walwyn).

Patricia Gillies has been a teacher for 26 years; married with one daughter and four stepchildren. Three of these have received an excellent classical education, and two of them have a degree in Classics.

Thomas Moore: Since I discovered Ficino in 1972, he has been my mentor and a strong influence in all my books and my way of life. We are both musicians, writers, translators, therapists, magicians, theologians, and lovers of beauty. I spend my days writing, composing music, and making things from wood. Where he had his circle of professional friends, my focus is on my family life. His notion of a Renaissance person, to which I aspire, is far more subtle than the popular image, and I trust that if we all shared his ideal, our society would recover the grace of which he spoke so precisely.

Dr. Charlotte Mendes da Costa qualified in medicine in 1991. She now works part-time as a general practitioner, and full-time as a wife and mother. She also studies at the School of Economic Science.

Noel Cobb is an archetypal psychotherapist. In 1987 he founded The London Convivium for Archetypal Studies, inspired by Ficino's Letter 42 in Volume 2. In 1993 he hosted a 5-day conference on the life and work of Ficino at the Villa Medici, Careggi, in Florence – splendidly covered in the journal *Sphinx* Vol. 6.

David Boddy worked as a political press secretary to the British Prime Minister, the Rt. Hon. Margaret Thatcher, in the 1979 and 1983 general elections, two of her greatest victories. He gained an insider's view of top political leadership, complementing in a very practical way his private studies into Marsilio Ficino. Subsequently, David has developed a number of communication companies, including Farsight Management, which specialises in top executive coaching and leadership development.

Professor Father Peter Serracino-Inglott is the former Rector and current Professor of Philosophy of the University of Malta and the recipient of many high international honours. As well as books and opera *libretti*, he has written numerous articles in the border areas between philosophy and the human sciences. He is a member of the editorial boards of several international journals including the *Journal of Mediterranean Studies*, *Arte Cristiana*, *Ethos*, and *Kos*.

Michael Shepherd is a writer, teacher and obituarist. For him, the compilation of this volume has been an education in itself, and he trusts that readers will echo his gratitude to the contributors for their generous participation in this quincentenary celebration.